RELIGION AND EDUCATION

ISLAMIC AND CHRISTIAN APPROACHES

Edited by

Syed Ali Ashraf
Paul H.Hirst

Foreword by

Anwar Ibrahim

The Islamic Academy
Cambridge

ISBN 0 948295 16 3

Published by
The Islamic Academy, Cambridge
23 Metcalfe Road, Cambridge CB4 2DB, U.K.

Printed by The Ipswich Book Company

Forthcoming Works

Religion and Education Series
General Editor: Syed Ali Ashraf

Other titles in this series

Science Education and Religious Beliefs

Faith-based Education in a Multi-faith Country

Islamic Curriculum Series
General Editor: Syed Ali Ashraf

Social Studies: Chief Editor, Syed Ali Ashraf
Vol I   : Introduction and Teaching Methodology
Vol II : Lesson Preparation: Ages 5-9
Vol III : Lesson Preparation: Ages 9-12

Natural Sciences: Author and Chief Editor, Shaikh Abdul Mabud
Vol I   : Introduction and Teaching Methodology
Vol II : Lesson Preparation: Ages 5-11
Vol III : Lesson Preparation: Ages 11-14
Vol IV : Lesson Preparation: Ages 14-16

Contents

Foreword

Fifteen years have passed since the First World Conference on Muslim Education was held in Makkah in 1977. Since then four other world conferences have been held. Muslim majority countries endorsed their recommendations at their foreign ministers' conferences. Even then they find it difficult to implement the recommendations mainly because education is a state subject and hence the education policy must be broad based enough to cater for the needs and requirements of all faith groups, even if we want to ignore the non-faith groups of these countries. What we needed was an assessment of these recommendations from a multi-faith and multi-cultural perspective. Islam is not a new religious tradition of the world. It is the final, most perfect and complete manifestation of the same truth that was revealed to earlier prophets. Is it not necessary then to think not only Islamically about the Muslims but also religiously about all the religious groups in the world today so that we use a common religious approach to education based on a common denomination of basic principles?

There are two other reasons for which this broad-based approach seems all the more necessary. The religious tradition of the world is overpowered by the secularist tradition. Even religion is studied from a secular point of view. Religion has been marginalised in such a way that God is eliminated from the universe, the spirit of a human being is totally ignored in favour of the psyche and the mind and all values are regarded as formulated by the society and hence relative to socio-cultural situation. Muslims have resisted this secularisation to some extent but the secularist education system has already done a lot of erosion. We shall not be able to stand up for any values at all. All values will become relative. Hence these values will be controlled by forces in different countries which would like to control the minds of people.

This leads to the second reason for a total emphasis on the religious sensibility of the human being. If the Muslims want to live as Muslims today, they cannot live in isolation. Is it not better then to have a religious atmosphere in the world rather than a secularist one?

Only through a dialogue with other religious groups on crucial issues can we have an atmosphere conducive to the cultivation of the religious sensibility. It is high time for all religious groups to get together to prepare an education policy that will ensure the sustenance of the religious sensibility in the country and at the same time give full scope to individual religious groups to maintain, preserve and further their individual religious cultures adequately. By holding a seminar on 'Faith as the Basis of Education in a Multi-faith Multi-cultural Country' The Islamic Academy of Cambridge has already taken a very bold stand in this direction.

The present work is the first book of its kind in which we shall get Islamic and Christian approaches to education as a whole, to literary education, to education in social science, especially social studies, and education in natural science. It is not an attempt to work out a formula from the lectures delivered at the University of Cambridge. It is an exploration into the unknown. But because of known territories and the common goal, it will be possible for the editors to attract the attention of other educationalists and stir the minds of all religious groups in this country and elsewhere.

His Excellency Anwar Ibrahim
(Ex-Education Minister of Malaysia)
Finance Minister of Malaysia

Preface

Since the First World Conference on Muslim Education held in
Makkah in 1977 there has been a campaign throughout the world
to 'Islamise' knowledge and to 'Islamise' education. In recent
years in England a new campaign has been launched by the
Christians to set up Christian schools. Both the groups speak the
same language in criticising the modern secular education system. What I said while preparing the Memorandum for the First
World Conference on Muslim Education has been echoed in *The
New Christian Schools* written by Ruth Deakin, the Director of the
Christian Schools Campaign and published in 1989. I criticised
the modern education system because it is based on a concept of
human nature which does not recognise the human spirit and its
relationship with God and thereby eliminates the possibility of
revelations and God-given knowledge and guidance for mankind. It is also based on a world view that propagates the concept
of society producing values and thereby creating a tradition of
values and a tradition of the evolution of values. This world view
is fundamentally of this world and hence it does not rouse in the
pupils' mind the slightest consciousness of life after death. It is
difficult to keep religious consciousness alive in the hearts of
children when all branches of knowledge are dominated by such
a view of life and when teachers are expected not to teach from
the religious point of view. For more than one hundred years
teacher training institutes and colleges have been propagating
this secularist approach. Even religious education is taught from
a non-religious secularist point of view, not from the point of view
of cultivating the religious sensibility. I therefore suggested and
the scholars at the First World Conference agreed to recommend
that research should be carried out to replace the secularist
concepts at the roots of all branches of knowledge by concepts
drawn from the Islamic frame of life and values as found in the
Qur'ān and the Sunnah.

I am glad to see that Ruth Deakin is using the same language
and the same concepts. She also finds the great majority of

schools is 'determined by a secularised view of life' and says:

> The dominance of this human-centred philosophy is evident throughout the whole of the curriculum and is frequently the implicit world-view which is being imparted to the children. As with all faiths or world-views, 'secular humanism' directs an individual's or a school's whole perspective on reality, shaping value systems and the philosophical framework from which all the disciplines are taught. And secular humanism finds expression in a wide variety of narrower perspectives on knowledge (such as rationalism, empiricism, naturalism and relativism), and on morality and society (such as Marxism, liberalism and functionalism). (p.5)

As a result she finds in schools a reflection of the society 'where there is increasing secularisation, a rising materialism and excessive individualism. Alongside this there is unremitting evidence of a profound lack of respect for authority, and chaos in the area of personal values and morality. There is an alarming increase in violent crime among young people and a disturbing lack of purpose in the lives of many people' (pp. 5 - 6). Schools, she rightly points out, are following 'a secularised curriculum' and promoting a particular philosophy of life. It is an irony, she says, 'that despite society's commendable desire to be truly multi-cultural, we are actually perpetuating a mono-cultural education system, and are denying children and their parents and philosophical pluralism which the coexistence of their various faiths would seem to require'. (p. 7)

I have gone a step further. As the struggle is between the secularist approach and the religious approach to life, I am trying to bring together all the important religions recognised in this country in order to maintain both unity and diversity. Unity lies in the concept of One Unique Supreme and Transcendental Reality which is the Deity or God in Judaism, Christianity, Islam, Hinduism and Sikhism and the Transcendental Reality in Buddhism, in the concept of the presence of a Spirit in each individual which is endowed with eternal values in potentiality and in the recognition of some form of Divine guidance. The

xii

diversity is maintained at the doctrinal level and at the socio-cultural level necessitating knowledge and understanding of each other and assimilation as far as possible of each other's diverse attitudes and approaches. In order to achieve this end it is necessary to have frank and free discussion among educationalists belonging to different religious groups. The Islamic Academy arranged a dialogue between Christian and Muslim educationalists in September 1989 entitled 'Faith as the Basis of Education in a Multi-faith Multi-cultural Country' and also organised in 1990 another seminar of the representatives of the six religions recognised in U.K. on the same topic. Both the seminars were highly successful. Discussion documents were produced as a result of these seminars. The Department of Education co-operated with the Academy in this project.

Prior to this seminar held in 1989 I organised two series of public lectures at the University of Cambridge in order to bring Christian and Muslim scholars and educationalists together. The first one entitled 'Religion as the Basis of Education' was held in 1983 and the second entitled 'Science Education and Religious Beliefs' in 1988. In the first series we had six topics and in the second series, we had four topics and each topic was handled by a Christian and a Muslim scholar. These two led the way to the seminar, 'Faith as the Basis of Education in a Multi-faith, Multi-cultural Country' held in 1989 and the success of this dialogue led to the seminar in which representatives of all the six religions participated.

Professor Paul Hirst, the then Head of the Department of Education of the University of Cambridge gave his full co-operation in arranging the first series of lectures and is the co-editor of the book that has come out of it. Professor David Hargreaves, the present Head of the Department of Education co-operated with me and the Department, as in the case of the previous series, co-sponsored along with the Islamic Academy in organising the second series of lectures entitled 'Science Education and Religious Beliefs'. On behalf of the Islamic Academy I acknowledge with gratitude their co-operation and encouragement.

I hope, the recent faith-based seminar will extend our area of co-operation and help the authorities not merely of the United Kingdom but also of the rest of the world to formulate an

Introduction

Paul H. Hirst

Education is, of its nature, concerned with the next generation's acquisition of many different kinds of understanding, beliefs, skills, values and attitudes, with societies and individuals seeking to hand on what they judge to be the best form of life. In many societies that form of life, down to its very particular details, has in the past been dominated by distinctive religious claims. In most societies today, however, that form of life is a much more complex matter, being a changing amalgam of elements that can be seen to come from long standing practical experience and the development of theoretical and practical reason as much as from some specific religious tradition. The validity and importance of the religious elements within any form of life have been challenged particularly in western societies and contemporary education has then come to be seen largely in secular terms. The developments of science and the ever expanding control over man and his environment which technology has made possible have progressively undermined many simplistic religious ideas. And further, the fact that the hugely impressive achievements of the sciences rest crucially on observation and experiment, open questioning and critical public tests has served to cast corrosive doubt on the validity and objectivity of all other claims to understanding and knowledge, particularly those of a religious nature. Not surprisingly education has therefore increasingly come to be formulated in non-religious terms and primarily as the development of rational autonomy. In this, what is handed on is above all a critical approach to all areas of human experience and

1

understanding and all presently accepted beliefs and practices are passed on as questionable and revisable.

This 'rationalism' in education has been presented by some as denying any legitimate role to religious considerations. Others have taken a more open ended view, seeing religious claims as expressions of a particular if distinctive rational pursuit which if it does not provide agreed conclusions, must at least be taken seriously by education. But even this more sympathetic view cannot build education on specific religious claims unless they conform to some concept of 'religious reason' and what that is remains a matter of wide dispute. A sceptical relativism or pluralism in religious matters thus seems the best that education can assume. And such a position has been underlined with the increasing religious pluralism of western multi-cultural societies. Democratic concerns for freedom and equality have led to an emphasis on education and schooling which has sought to evade or play down the significance of religious beliefs even when they are accepted as of cultural concern and interest.

The validity of this 'rationalistic' view of education is, however, now itself coming under more careful scrutiny. It is questioned whether religious scepticism or agnosticism must be taken as the only legitimate 'rational' conclusion on religious matters. Is not commitment to a specific religious tradition with all that that implies, at least as legitimate a conclusion, and must not education therefore build seriously on specific beliefs? The strong articulation of contemporary Islam and the endeavour to approach the sciences and the arts in Islamic terms is providing a sharp focus for this re-appraisal. The revival of a more fundamentalist approach amongst Christians of many denominations adds force to these concerns. We are therefore going through a period of uncertainty and debate amongst philosophers and religious thinkers that is a major educational import. What is at stake is clarifying the relationship between religious beliefs, the wide ranging content of contemporary education and the organisation of education in contemporary society.

It is as a contribution to current debate on these matters that this volume of papers by distinguished academics and scholars is to be seen. It is based on a series of public lectures given under the auspices of the University of Cambridge Department of Education and the Islamic Academy, Cambridge, and seeks to address six of the most basic questions in this area from a Christian and an Islamic point of view. Starting with the issue of the foundation of education the papers then consider in turn the significance of religious values in the pursuit and study of the sciences, literature and the social sciences. The distinctive significance of specifically moral and religious elements in education are then examined from these two points of view prior to a final pair of papers respectively on Islamic and Christian education in the state maintained school system of the United Kingdom. In all these contributions the writers express their own personal judgements and there is divergence of opinion amongst both Christian and Muslim authors. No unanimity of view can at present be expected on many of these issues here addressed either amongst Muslims or Christians, let alone between these groups. But the debates religious thinkers are here engaged in are undeniably of major contemporary importance. It is hoped that this collection will help promote their consideration at a fundamental level by both those who can share certain of the authors' religious convictions and those who find them altogether unacceptable.

Can Education Have a Religious Foundation Today?

An Islamic Approach

Hasan Askari

Education involves a twofold process of conscious teaching and learning. Consciousness involves not only the knowledge of the method and the findings of a given discipline but also the awareness of the structure of assumptions on which the methodolgy of that discipline is based. The most important question to be asked at the very outset of this paper is whether the teacher really knows *what* he is teaching, though he is quite aware that he is teaching psychology or sociology, philosophy or history, biology or astronomy. Does he know in what particular world-view his teaching of one or another subject is located? To know this is to practise conscious education. We are not at this stage concerned whether the world-view in question is right or wrong. What we are stressing as the first essential requirement in any educational undertaking is whether those who are participating in it are conscious of the underlying philosophy of their method and curriculum. To become conscious is to become objective. The philosophy, however one upholds it, is now an object of inquiry. It is no longer a hidden assumption, no longer something to be taken for granted uncritically. Like the particular data of a given discipline, the philosophy which underlies its methodology is now an object of open study. Hence, there is a world

5

of difference between conscious and unconscious education.

The ideal situation is one when the teacher is both
conscious and objective regarding the underlying philosophy of his educational system. However desirable, this is
rare. This is however facilitated when the intellectual universe of a given society entertains more than one philosophy so that a dialogue is possible between different philosophies. Though they might be conflicting and irreconcilable
as is the case between the materialistic and the religious
schools of thought, they, by their very co-presence, engender a certain degree of objectivity towards their own basic
assumptions. This is workable when neither of them is absolutely dominant as ideologies. All this rests on how far
the schools of thought in dialogue respect the principle of
the intellectual freedom of the individual.

Can education have a religious foundation today? The
question presupposes that the answer one way or the other
will be respected. If there is only one answer, it will then
mean that it is a closed society, and in that case the question
itself will not arise. The very fact that it has arisen is a sign
of hope, for a free discussion is possible, and a free discussion as such, irrespective of its outcome, is a proof that the
human spirit is free. As I intend to answer the question in
the affirmative, I shall try to put forth the religious viewpoint remaining aware all the time that like any other point
of view it is tentative, all too human, for to remember this
is the very demand of my religious conscience, for to be
modest with regard to even the strongly held religious
convictions is the only way to remember the Immensity of
the Transcendental and Inscrutable Reality.

Can education have a religious foundation today? The
question has a date. What does 'today' mean? The historical
aspect of the question involves an ambiguity. The obvious
reference in the question is however simple that education
did have a religious foundation in the past but in the

present times it has a non-religious or even anti-religious basis. The entire drive in our times is to secularize education and to keep it away from any religious influence. There appears to be a clear conflict between the scientific method on which the present education is based and the religious outlook which is supposed to obstruct free and critical inquiry without which modern education cannot possibly be conceived. All this could be easily questioned, but at this stage we are concerned more with the historicity of the question. What is the significance of 'today'? What sort of reference is it? When did it begin? How long will it last? Will there be a "tomorrow" for this "today" when it will be a "yesterday"? None of these questions could be answered concerning this 'today', for it is not a reference to any meaningful temporal dimension. It is a mythical image of the ideology of 'modern times', and rests on a highly ambiguous idea of history which lacks existential content. A creation of Marx and Spengler, a history without memory, a structure that is imposed on the concrete experience of man, a history which is inbuilt in the modern disciplines of economics, politics and sociology, has nothing to do with life, for it has no individual or collective memory of any man or nation. One can write the history of India from a Marxian or a Spenglarian point of view without referring at any stage to the actual lives of the people of India, their beliefs, their festivals, their arts and crafts, their heroes, their visions and dreams, their loyalties to tradition, their births and deaths. There is always a meeting of the past, present and future in the concrete lives of men and women. There is no such thing as irreversibility of time in the life of the spirit. The past is reenacted; the present is enlarged to include eternity, and the future comes by the route of the past. A modern historian following one or another philosophy of history current in our times is quite incapable of comprehending the enactment of "Eucharist" each Sunday or the "Ashura" each Muharram, and the "Passover" each year, for

7

he has no basis in his method to grapple with this kind of handling of history in the actual religious and emotional life of millions of people. For him there is past barred and closed, bygone once for all, and a present whose authority he places above everything else, and if he is questioned from where this authority is derived, he has no answer. Hence, there is something not merely wrong but pathological in his conception of historical time. Hence, I hesitate to take the historical aspect of the question on its face value. There is an implicit judgement against the past in the modern understanding of the present. The way in which we understand time is crucial for it decides the course of our development both morally and spiritually. It has far-reaching consequences for education itself. The kind of history which the modern mind seems to offer cannot possibly support education itself, for education presupposes an enterprise of generations of mankind. There is a vast participation of the people of past in every discourse which goes on in a class room or seminar of today. It is this unity and life of knowledge across centuries which gives to education its spiritual character. Historical barriers are always transcended by both the teacher and the pupil. Hence, we need to restate the question in basically different terms. Can we have education with a philosophy of history as one of its foundations, a philosophy which on one side has nothing to do with the concrete lives and memories of mankind, and on the other does not have any conception of the unity of time? It is however not without significance to refer to 'today' in our question but its significance is not the same for a Marxist and a Muslim. For the latter, the "day" (*al-yawm*) has both a temporal significance in the ordinary sense of the word and also a prophetic and eschatological significance. Hence, to speak of anything in purely modern terms, in terms of time, without a prophetic and eschatological sense, is almost an impossibility for a Muslim, for he is contemporary not only to this day, but also to other days, the days of his Prophet, to all the Days of the Revelation of God. Once, when we utter "God", we relate ourselves to more than one time. Hence, when I accept the historical terms of the question, I accept it tentatively for purposes of dialogue in the meaning in which those who have no conception of prophetic and eschatological time use it, but all the time when I say 'today' I involve all eternity.

Education as it is understood in a non-religious sense has three basic points of departure: (1) scientific method, (2) suspension of judgement on claims made by religions, and (3) pragmatism. Those who violate the second principle and take an aggresive stand against all religions go beyond what the scientific approach requires of them, and thus turn education into a tool for a materialistic and secular ideology. To provide a religious foundation for education does not mean that its scientific foundation should be removed. An Islamic approach does not rest on the notion of conflict between science and religion. A religious foundation, from an Islamic point of view, will mean not the abolition of the scientific foundation but its continuation under the vigilance of a religious critique and its limitation to areas where science has every right to be sovereign. The religious critique operates at the frontier where there is a constant danger of science becoming a thorough materialistic ideology.

But the relationship between scientific method and materialistic ideology is a highly complex matter. The religious critique may degenerate into a simplistic statement of conflict between itself and scientific-materialistic approach in terms of divine revelation and human reason, or an apologetic equation between religion and reason. The religious critique of the Western scientific and materialistic ideology has to go to the very depth of the matter, namely, the very basic assumptions of the scientific method, because it is the basic structure of thought on which science rests which ultimately admits of a materialistic approach.

9

Long before Marx and Nietzsche, it was Descartes who laid the foundations of an approach which led to the destruction of the religious understanding of man. It was not his method as applied in natural sciences but his well-known statement "Cogito ergo sum" which revolutionised the Western thought and took it far away from its religious foundations. Descartes fell into an heroic fallacy when he assumed that the same subject who asks a question and raises a doubt solves the problem. He identified the majestic "I" of God in his soul who asked a response from him as the responsive "you" from whom the answer was wrested. He labelled the two speakers with a single ambiguous term, "ego". This self-conversing personality is an invention of the modern times. Thus, this unreal I, the ego, once manufactured, God, Man and World all three collapsed. The Cartesian announcement ran in direct encounter with the cry of Jesus on the Cross: "Eli eli, lama sabachthani?" By that cry the limits were established between divinity and humanity, and by the Cartesian statement the limits were abolished in favour of a lonely, ambiguous "ego". Long before God "died" on the lips of Nietzsche, he was expelled from the human heart. Descartes could not realise that all great questions are put to us by a power which far transcends our consciousness and free will, and it is in responding to those questions that we become "religious". But the word of Descartes had to go on unquestioned. A world of thought sprang up from Marx to Spencer, from Nietzsche to Freud. None of these systems were possible without the Cartesian "ego". To provide a religious foundation to education will then mean taking the enormous step of saying farewell to Descartes for ever.

It will also mean turning away from all those systems of thought which flourished on the Cartesian foundations. A sense of emptiness will definitely set in, and exasperation too. But we cannot go on with the Cartesian approach having once discovered the grand fallacy. This will inevitably imply the choice for a spiritual anthropology, for a religious conception of man, for that man who carries in his heart an ongoing dialogue between his finite self and his Infinite Lord who made him, and breathed His Spirit into him, a dialogue when it is in the heart of the Elect of God, when objectified, becomes "a revelation revealed".

This Man is the Mystic Man capable of transcending the limitations imposed on the species by its material nature. He is the individual who possesses the vision of a transcendental Reality. This brings us to the very concept of religion itself. It appears easy when it is contrasted with materialism, but what about religions themselves? Do they have a common conception of what they mean by religion? The religious critique should now be directed against its own house, for here is another set of problems. If by religion we mean our own tradition which is superior to all other religions and which is the final truth to be revealed, and if by the religious foundations of education we mean only an Islamic or only a Christian foundation, we confuse faith with belief, guidance with doctrine, and orientation with ritual. We have to make distinctions between different contents of religion, different levels of religious consciousness, and different forms of religion within each religion. We have to distinguish, interrelate, generalize. Standing within our respective traditions we can rise to a higher level within our own tradition and communicate with people of similar levels of development in other religious traditions. We have to draw the boundaries of salvation in some other way, other than those of our respective historical-collective identities. We have to provide to modern education an inter-religious foundations. We have to simplify, universalize and intensify this foundation. This will involve separating form from content. This will imply a real testimony of God's Oneness, transcendence and universality. The Islamic contribution towards this end is in terms of four convictions:

(1) There is no god but God. The crucial affirmation should precede with a clear and consistent negation of every false absolute, whether it be of religion, race, lan-

11

guage, or of country, and above all else, the negation of the "ego", the strongest of all the false absolutes;

(2) There is only One God, God of all mankind; there is no other. We have moved away from the "gods" of this or that country or city. There is no such thing as a Christian or a Muslim God, for God is one, and He is on all sides. How else could God be? Of course, we have different names and varying understandings of God. And it should be so, for if God is equated absolutely with one particular form of understanding, He is then that Form, not God. Herein lies the mystery of the Islamic notion of *subḥāniyyah* that He is above all we say of Him. But being universal, being transcendent, being contemporary to all times, He is closer to all of us than our own selves. It is this intimacy which is a secret (*sirr*) between God and the individual, which is beyond description. For men and women of intense religious awareness, God is a Fact much more Real and Intimate than the fact of their consciousness of themselves, for He is the Consciousness of consciousness;

(3) We are of God, and unto God we return. Of course, our body is from this earth; our food is drawn from it; the light which our eyes require is from this heaven; and yet we are not from this world; for our country is God, unto Him we all are returning, knowingly and unknowingly. It is this Godwardness, this orientation, this *qiblah*, which is what has to be provided as the central content of our self-awareness.

(4) There are only two 'days' in the Islamic 'time' - the Day of Covenant (*mithāq*) when on the dawn of creation we all said, "Yes", when we were asked, "Am I not your Lord?" Another Day will be that when we shall all assemble before Him, when all will come 'home'. And between these two 'days' there is the 'night' of this world, and we keep the lamp of the Prophetic Revelation burning, drawing from it both light and warmth. There is thus a unity of the first and the last, of creation and eschatology. It is by remembering God, our real origin, our First Day and our Last Day that we become truly human. It is the unity of reflection and contemplation on the One Reality that is God that should become the foundation of our education.

Can Education Have a Religious Foundation Today ?

A Christian View

Peter J Mitchell

Education is a term beset with ambiguities.[1] It is possible to use it in a purely descriptive way when referring to the whole or part of the upbringing of children. So Locke employs the term when he remarks, 'of all men we meet with - nine parts of them are what they are, good or evil, useful or not, by their education.' Hume does the same when, more pessimistically, he perceives of education 'as the source of our confused and irrational beliefs' and we do likewise when we attribute to someone a good or bad education. Or education can be spoken of in straight forward institutional terms, when, for example, we speak of the educational system of England and Wales or the financial cost of state education. Thirdly, we can employ the term in a much more strictly evaluative sense when we try to pick out those procedures and practices which we hope will result in truly 'educated person' and which will thus help us to decide what kind of upbringing and institutions we ought to provide for the proper education of our young.

It follows, therefore, that in enquiring if a religious foundation for education is possible today, we may be asking one or more of the following questions:-

1. Can the upbringing of children in the twentieth century be guided by religious principles and beliefs or

inspired by a religious point of view?

2. Should any schools or similar institutions in our present society be given a religious foundation in that decisions about their organisation, structure and curriculum would be decisively influenced by religion?

3. Can we legitimately formulate our educational objectives in terms of a particular religious perspective, as, for example, did Arnold when he spoke of the purpose of education in his school being the production of 'Christian gentlemen and scholars', or T.S. Eliot when he advocated that education should encourage 'the development of wisdom and holiness'?[2]

Why however, do such questions about education arise? They come, surely, from that central fact about human beings upon which the various possibilities of upbringing, educational institutions and evaluative decisions themselves depend. That is, the rather obvious point that we do not spring fully clothed and armed into the world, immediately ready to enter life's fray. Instead we are born totally dependant upon adults. We lack speech and powers of locomotion. We have to be provided with food, warmth and security. Whatever the capacities and potentialities we may be born with, we come into the world totally ignorant. We are, of course, alive with all that means for the young infant, but for all practical purposes everything has to be acquired; language, customs, knowledge, skills, attitudes and beliefs. The mind, we say, is not yet formed, the body underdeveloped. There is a process of maturation through which all must go. Of course we are not just 'tabula rasa' as Locke is supposed to have assumed. We have to become active and lively agents in learning. And to be fair to Locke, he too believed that the child's spirit should be kept 'easy, active and free'.

Yet though the infant may be born ignorant, the social world into which he comes is rich in knowledge and intellectual and cultural achievements. It is all too easy in decrying the barbarities and conflicts of our present age to underestimate the value of the glittering prizes offered by human civilisation. The heritage that is the child's by right is filled with treasures of almost incalculable wealth. It would be almost criminal and certainly a serious form of deprivation to deny him access to this accumulation of wisdom and understanding gained over many millenia and embodied in innumerable forms of social life.

But however praiseworthy and attractive they may seem, mankind's cultural and cognitive attainments have about them an ineradicable flaw. For the ignorance of the infant is not just a transient stage in his development, easily outgrown. It is a permanent feature of the human condition. Aristotle apparently thought that our knowledge of the empirical world would soon be completed. He was, it seems, mistaken. Indeed, the possibility and even the necessity of revision, correction and reinterpretation in the light of fresh evidence and changed circumstances lie at the heart of the human intellectual quest. Nor is ignorance our only defect. Moral weakness and social disharmony seem to be inescapale features of our corporate existence.

Whilst, therefore, the upbringing of children necessarily involves passing on something from this immense store of human accomplishments, it cannot be a blind handing on of what has been received. We have to pay proper attention to the possibility of error and moral turpitude, and provide the child with those intellectual skills and moral qualities which will enable him to cope with such difficulties and perhaps in his turn be able to add to the sum of human wisdom.

Further, what is passed on to the child is not external to him, like possessions and money. The knowledge, skills and attitudes he gains have to be internalised. They have to become part of him, and in doing so they help to transform him. Through their acquisition he gradually becomes a different person. Thus an upbringing that involves initiating children into their intellectual inheritance is also unavoidably concerned with helping them to develop as persons, with their own distinctive characters, likes and dislikes, aptitudes and interests. This influence is further accentuated by the child's need to evolve his own life style and modes of relating to others, things which have to be culled mainly from the various models presented to him. Thus in the upbringing of children, no matter how much we may wish to provide children with the maximum freedom to grow in the way that they themselves see fit, we cannot avoid both directly and indirectly helping to give form to persons.

Of course, some upbringers may hesitate to provide much freedom. But they can only hinder and never totally stop a process that in normal circumstances is inexorable. For children grow up, they no longer need their parents. Indeed, their parents often come to need them. The pupil becomes independent of the teacher. In upbringing, even though sometimes it may appear to the contrary, we are increasingly concerned not only with initiating children into ways of knowledge and understanding, but also as time passes with handing over power and influence. Eventually everything is involved. Human mortality sees to that.

Upbringing, however, is not a value free activity. It does not proceed in an automatic fashion. Innumerable choices and decisions have to be made. What, for example, ought we to pass on? It could hardly be everything. Few parents would want to pass on a liking for violence or an addiction to torture or drugs. We try to induct children into what we see as valuable and appropriate rather than what is harmful or dangerous. And if we are helping to form persons, we can hardly do this without having any notion as to what kind of person we think this should ideally be. Even if we are unthinking followers of tradition, it is inevitable that our activities will either directly or indirecly provide some model for emulation, and therefore exclude commending some other model, whether we like it or not. And our manner of handing over power and influence as well as the kind of social perceptions we give to the child will carry just as many value implications.

It is not hard to see how the religious believer will approach these fundamental value questions involved in the upbringing of children. His religious convictions will inevitably mould to a lesser or greater extent what he sees as valuable and wishes to pass on to his children. And his beliefs will almost certainly entail some pattern of personal development and social interactions that he will wish to commend and encourage. He have not act in a coercive or irrational fashion. We have to remember that many religions, at least officially, so abhor compulsion in questions of faith that they mark the acceptance of personal responsibility for one's own beliefs and actions with distinctive religious ceremonies. Nevertheless, the religious beliefs he affirms, the religious practices he engages in and the religious duties he undertakes must mark the way the believer both understands and carries out the task of upbringing of his children. However much his critics may demur and however difficult he finds the task to carry out in practice, he has to respond to our first question in the affirmative. He is morally bound to guide the upbringing of his children by means of his own religious beliefs and convictions. He is scarcely able to do otherwise, without first in an important sense jettisoning his religion. And it would be extraordinary, if not a contradiction in terms, if a 'free society' required him in an important area of his life to do this.

Yet it is here that the upbringing of children in a religious tradition seems to come into direct conflict with education understood in both an institutional and an evaluative sense. For the freedom that guarantees the believer's right to practise his religion also exposes it to opposition and criticism. His system of belief is only one amongst many, and no matter how firm his own convictions and however strongly he holds to their truth, his faith and certainty are not shared by all. And he has to live in a society where these divisions are glaringly apparent, and whose educational system has to come to terms with this intractible diversity, a problem not easy of solution. For the more an institution such as a school embodies the attitudes, beliefs and practices of one particular view point, whether it be religious or not, the more partisan and socially divisive it will appear to be. Yet if it attempts to reflect a multitude of diverse and perhaps contradictory world views, the more incompatible it will be with the ideals and values of any one particular religious group. To this problem we will have to return.[3] But even if some administrative compromise can be reached and we can arrive at some modus vivendi which allows the institutions to function in a way that causes the least possible social damage or religious offence, we are still left with the challenge presented by education understood in its more evaluative mode.

Where the perimeters of education are to be drawn and what constitutes a truly educated person are matters of some dispute. But however widely or narrowly we draw the map, and whatever weight we give to the place of the creative and effective arts, life skills and social responsibilities, there seems to be an irreducible core in education that is concerned with the pursuit of knowledge. 'Education', it is claimed, 'means in part at least that children are to be initiated into worthwhile fields of knowledge and experience in ways that will enable them to distinguish truth from falsity, opinion from fact, the authentic from the inauthentic'. And if this is at all successful it means that the child will 'increasingly be guided in his thoughts and actions not by social pressures from without, nor by the unreflections of uncontrolled emotions and desires within', but, as it were,

18

by the cool voice of reason. That is, the process of education should both respect and help incresingly to develop as the child gets older, his own personal rational autonomy. He will no doubt often be guided by the wisdom and knowledge of others, but in principle at least, he will learn to take responsibility for his own views and to be guided in his beliefs and actions by the freely arrived at perceptions of his own mind.[4]

This view of education has two important corollaries. Firstly, the forms of knowledge and experience, which are to be the vehicles of this educational achievement, possess in an important respect their own independence as autonomous modes of discourse. And this entails, for example, that what makes a good mathematician is not his ideological commitment but his capacity to do mathematics. Similarly, scientific procedures remain the same whoever operates them. Coupled to this is the second and equally important principle that there must be some non-arbitrary way of deciding between questions of truth and falsity and illusion and reality in these fields of discourse; some objective tests that are not dependent on personal whim or subjective opinion, to which knowledge claims in that particular field have to be subjected, and only if they pass can they claim to have been substantiated. Without these twin pillars of relatively independent modes of intellectual discourse and non-aribtrary methods of authentication, the pursuit of knowledge that is claimed to lie at the heart of the educational endeavour would, it is asserted, be largely impossible, no matter how we eventually decide to draw our epistemological map.

At first sight this may not worry the religious believer as little of it seems to be incompatible with the kind of upbringing he seeks for his young. To most Christians at least and to many other religious believers as well, the world is fundamentally intelligible, open to independent investigation and subject in principle if not in practice to human use and control. Admittedly the doctrine of creation goes much further than that. For it also sees the world as a gift to humankind to be lived in with responsibility and reverence and involves the idea of human dependence on God and the conviction that the more the believer perceives and understands the complexities of the universe, the more intense and total will be his worship of a benificent creator. 'The heavens tell out the glory of God, the vault of heaven reveals his handiwork'. (Psalm 19)

Far, therefore, from being alien to the religious perspective, the ideas of autonomous forms of knowledge and non-arbitrary means of verification would seem to be necessary prolegomena to such an understanding of human existence. Similarly the freedom of the individual achieved through rational autonomous thought and behaviour can itself be seen in terms of a religious virtue, especially where the pre-eminence of conscience and belief in personal responsibility are prized. As Vatican II somewhat paradoxically empressed it, 'The exercise of religion consists before all else in those internal voluntary and free acts whereby man sets the course of his life directly towards God'. Such a response would be impossible if a person had not in an important sense become an autonomous agent.

Seen in this light education and the religious upbringing of children are not incompatible but contiguous activities, sharing similar goals and values and both enriching each other. If this were true there would be no need to look for a religious foundation for education. It would exist in its own right and stand on its own feet, though it would also form a necessary and welcome part of the religious upbringing of children rightly understood.

Unfortunately the relationship between education and religion is not so easily construed. For education as it is outlined above, with its commitment to reason and evidence, implicitly claims to subject religion itself to critical appraisal. No easy going partnership is therefore possible.

This is especially true when we remember that there are any number of religious and non-religious world views and that no one of them can justifiably claim a privileged position granting exemption from this intellectual interrogation.

One way of responding to this challenge is to accept that education will inevitably make religion part of its subject matter, but claim that religion in turn should be entitled to offer an alternative vision to that propagated by a totally secular approach to education, a vision that would itself have to be able to be defended in an intellectually respectable fashion. Religion would thus have more of a prophetic than a foundational role in its relationship with education. Thus, for example, in response to the secular ideals of knowledge and goodness, the objectives of education could be redefined in T.S. Eliot's terms of wisdom and holiness. Admittedly we need knowledge and understanding, but we must go further and seek wisdom, and 'the fear of the Lord is the beginning of wisdom'. And man, it is claimed, needs more than goodness, for not only is he related to his fellows but also to God, and so requires holiness.

However, further objections to religion can be raised that would qualify even more its position in education. For not only is religion seen as part of the subject matter of education rather than its foundation, it is also seen as radically contentious in nature. There are, it is said, no publicly agreed objective tests by which religious claims can be justified. Schools, therefore, might and perhaps ought to, study religions as important phenomena in the world in which we live. But because of their controversial and disputed status it would be an illegitimate objective of education to attempt to bring about commitment to them or advocate that any one set of religious claims are true. Schools and similar institutions, it is asserted, ought therefore to remain totally neutral so far as questions of religion are concerned. They are, however, able to continue the tasks of education because of the autonomous nature of the fields of study with which they are primarily concerned.

Whether such a totally neutralist stance is possible is very much an open question. For it is all too easy to slide into another and more decisively secular mode of thinking about education. In it autonomy is not merely seen as ensuring that human beings learn to think for themselves, but it also entails that they depend totally on themselves. Such a view has a long history. So Bacon speaks of knowledge as power and the proposed aim of his New Academy is 'the enlargement of the bounds of human empire to the effecting of all things possible.' And John White recently expressed a similar view which he directly contrasts with a religious one. 'Today many would hold the very different view that our well being is of our own making. This is a man-centred picture, not a God-centred one. It bids fair to dominate educational thought as it has philosophical'.[5] This view need not be totally limited to the cognitive. One of the most eloquent expositions that recognises this can be found in Bertrand Russell's autobiography where he writes, 'Three passions, simple but overwhelmingly strong have governed my life: the longing for love, the search for knowledge and unbearable pity for the suffering of mankind'.[6] But its message is the same, the dignity of autonomous man is that he stands alone, free, rational, responsible and even brave, guided by his own conscience and the voice of his own reason.[7]

It is a very different picture of man to that portrayed in the Psalms.

> Where can I escape from thy spirit
> Where can I flee from thy presence
> If I climb up to heaven thou art there
> If I make my bed in Sheol again I find thee
> If I take my flight to the frontiers of the morning or
> dwell at the limits of the Western Sea,
> even there thy hand will meet me and thy right hand
> will hold me fast.[8]

Even more does it contrast with the response of the prophet Isaiah in the Jerusalem Temple, who awe struck by the vision of the holiness of Yahweh, cries out,

> Woe is me! I am lost
> For I am a man of unclean lips
> and I dwell amongst a people of unclean lips
> Yet with these eyes I have seen the King, the Lord of Hosts.[9]

Here is concept of human imperfection that calls for repentance which in this view extends far beyond the moral. As Michael Foster remarks of this passage in 'Mystery and Philosophy', 'The holiness of God is what makes man repent: indeed it cannot be recognised without repentance,' and 'when the intellect is faced with God it must be seized with a conviction of intellectual inadequacy parallel to the moral inadequacy with which we more commonly identify a sense of sin'.[10]

I am not here concerned with the truth or falsity of these two positions so much as the nature of the beliefs involved. Neither seem expressed with any sense of doubt. Indeed, doubt would be alien in such contexts. It does not make much sense to ask if Russell doubted his guiding passions or Isaiah his need to repent. The clash between them seems much more like the clash between two entirely different ways of looking at the world. They would, I suspect, be mutually incomprehensible to each other. The situation looks very much like the one discussed by Wittgenstein as reported in his Lectures on Religious Belief. 'Supose somebody made this guidance for his life: believing in the Last Judgement. Whenever he does anything this is before his mind.... He is held in the grip of a picture which regulates the whole of his life,[11] a picture which Wittgenstein admits he cannot at all understand. It was not, we might say, part of his world.

Iris Murdock makes a similar point when she is discussing fundamental differences in morals. Here, she says, 'moral differences look less like differences of choice given the same facts and more like differences of vision, a total difference of Gestalt. We differ not only because we select different objects out of the same world, but because we see different worlds'.[12]

The move from believing we inhabit one conceptual world to accepting there are many and sometimes incompatible worlds can perhaps also be seen occurring in Wittgenstein, who in the *Tractatus* asserts that everything which can be known, can be expressed in the propositions of science. Besides that there is the mystical which is inexpressible.[13] But in the *Investigations* he claims, 'What has to be accepted, the given is - so one could say - forms of life'.[14] But can we say anything about the structure of these different worlds, these fundamental forms of life, that makes them inhabitable? The first thing to remark is that they are social, they are not idiosyncratic and individual. To live in a world totally of your own making would be to be insane. Stewart Sutherland has suggested some further criteria.[15] Such a form of life would have to be related to detectable changes in behaviour. It must be lived or liveable. There must also be ways in it of distinguishing between coherence and incoherence. The language employed must not lapse into the ramblings of a fevered mind; the behaviour involved must have a point. There must be within it ways of distinguishing between truth and falsehood and between appearance and reality. And it must contain sufficient diversity and coherence so that it makes sense to use phrases like 'having something to live by'. We ought also to be able to draw inferences as to what is and is not compatible with the form of life. We might add that more successful forms of life would also be marked by cognitive fruitfulness, a capacity to throw light on an increasing range of phenomena and with a sufficient flexibility to cope with changing circumstances.

There is, therefore, a complex logical geography that would need to be mapped out fully to express the complexities of such a notion, and it would be inevitable that there would be many things that could be said that would only make full sense to those who, as it were, were on the inside. However, two more general points can be made. Firstly, there is the historical particularity implicit in this point of view. Such worlds or comprehensive forms of life are not intended to be mere theoretical constructs. They are essentially something that is lived. They have a context and a history which often involves complex developments, conflicts and interacting relationships. Secondly, there is no Olympian height from which they can be criticized, no independent way in which they can be measured. Of course, critics can arise from within. And such worlds can disintegrate. 'Forms of life are no longer lived.' Or they can be interrogated from other worlds, though this is no easy matter and profound misunderstandings can follow.

What, however, of those autonomous activities such as science with which education is supposed to be primarily concerned? Are they not ways of transcending this cultural entrapment? Here we need to distinguish between procedures and practices. A procedure such as that embodied in the scientific method can as a theoretical construct certainly be considered as autonomous, and therefore in some senses be thought of as culturally free. But before it can become a practice, that is, an activity actually engaged in, it must have a location. For before we can actually use the procedure we have to answer a host of what are largely value questions. For example, 'On what subject matter can the procedures be employed? Who shall engage in them - anyone? How shall the results be treated - open to all? Are the consequences of their use either desirable or acceptable? Who shall foot the bill? For this reason the practice of science can take a very different shape in different cultural contexts. Of course, this concept of location is a very complex one. It can be both cognitive – what is its fit in the total world view, etc? and social - what shall be its intstitutional setting or the status of its practitioners, etc? It is also possible that in some worlds a procedure such as science could have no place. There would be no cognitive or social room to allow for its location. And procedures can be borrowed, sometimes with disastrous results, though more normally they work in a cognitively fruitful way, helping to transform a particular world's perceptions.

If, therefore, we inhabit different worlds, what of education? It cannot exist in a free floating, cultureless way. For it too has to be part of a particular world. Its location as an evaluative procedure would be to ensure that the upbringing of children is properly related to the practices, character models and ways of power sharing which that world considered appropriate and valuable.

If this is true, it is easy to see how in a particular world education could have religious foundation. It would be where the practices, character models and ways of power sharing are informed to a lesser or greater extent by religious perceptions. Similarly, in a world conceived of in secular terms education would not nor could have a religious foundation.

Does this mean, however, that we are all locked into our own world, irredeemably committed to cultural and cognitive relativism, made worse because each world seems inexorably drawn to the belief that all other worlds are wrong or illusions?

This does not necessarily follow. Firstly, we have already referred to the fact that world views of this kind, embedded as they are in practices, have an historical particularity. They arise, flourish and die in space-time, and thus inevitably have some connections with each other. None spring ready made into a cultural vacuum. We can, therefore, trace out their histories, and see their inter-relationships as well as their differences, even if we have to do this from one particular points of view. And this historical interlocking can provide some points of mutual comprehension, though it is equally possible to be misled and profoundly mistaken by historical proximity.

Secondly, there are between worlds what can be called structural resemblances. Again it is easy to be misled, for what can be said in this area must of necessity come from the point of view of a particular world. There can be no independent or free standing analysis. However, we do all share in some ways a common humanity, even if our perceptions of what it is to be human differ profoundly. We are all physically born, grow old and physically die. There has to be some form of child upbringing. We all suffer pain, breathe, use languages, require food, shelter and sleep and have relationships with others. And between some worlds there are closer structural connections than that. These common features mean that when we attempt to speak across worlds, we are not talking to total strangers.

Thirdly, we do not live in isolation. For better or worse, differing worlds meet and increasingly and on a larger scale as techniques of communication and travel improve. But the results of such encounters can be mutual incomprehension and hostility, leading to conflict, or else they can result in some kind of dialogue, however tenuous and hesitant this might be.

We ought, therefore, to add to the aims of education, or to the work of such institutions as schools, the further task of facilitating this dialogue. This ought to be seen not as an optional extra but as an essential component of education, especially if we believe that the pursuit of knowledge is an indispensable element of education and also accept that humankind inhabits differing cognitive worlds. It would be a duty laid upon all schools whatever their foundation or cultural and ethnic mix.

How such a dialogue is to be facilitated lies beyond the brief of this eassy and involves much more than education and schools can provide. But it is, nevertheless, an essential part of education because, firstly, the ability to carry on such a dialogue is something to be learnt, and secondly, the implications of what lies behind the need for dialogue can affect almost all the activities carried on in school. Implicitly, it ought to influence the general life, organisation, rules and customs of the school, for these will say as much about the institution's general attitude to dialogue as will the more explicit teaching that is also required. So, implicitly, dialogue begins when a school treats seriously the customs, attitudes, beliefs and practices of all its members. And more explicitly the curriculum ought at some stage to allow for what Ninian Smart has called world view analysis, though how this is to be carried out is another and longer story.

However, it is important not to underestimate the difficulties entailed in such dialogues, nor conceal from ourselves the full implications of what is intended. Even the concept of dialogue will be understood differently in different worlds. And perhaps in some worlds there is as yet no location for such a notion. It may also require certain qualities such as patience, tolerance, trust, humility and courage, which need to be mutually understood before much progress can be made, though it may well be that such qualities could at first be shown by only one side. Engaging in dialogue may, therefore, demand some considerable sacrifices. Indeed, there is sometimes a need for what can only be called unilateral metaphysical disarmament, with all the dangers that implies, for dialogue even to have a chance of beginning. However, the alternative seems more frightening. In an age of balancing nuclear terror the difficulties of dialogue seem better than the carnage of conflict.

Notes

1. Cp. J. Passmore, *The Philosophy of Teaching*, p.21f.
2. T.S. Eliot, *The Idea of a Christian Society and Other Writings* (Second Edition) pp. 148 ff.
3. See page 15.
4. Cp. P.H. Hirst and R.S. Peters *The Logic of Education* pp. 17ff. et al.
5. John White, *The Aims of Education Restated*, p.37.
6. Bertrand Russell, *Autobiography*, Vol 1, Introduction.
7. Cp. Iris Murdock, *The Sovereignty of Good*, p. 80.
8. Psalm 139.
9. Isaiah Ch. 6 verse 5.
10. Michael B. Foster, *Mystery and Philososphy*, p. 46.
11. Wittgenstein, *Lectures and Conversations on Aesthetics, Psychology and Religious Belief,* pp. 53 ff.
12. Iris Murdock, 'Vision and Choice in Morality' in *Christian Ethics and Contemporary Philosophy,* ed., I.T. Ramsey, p. 203.
13. Cp. Wittgenstein, *Tractatus Logico-Philosophicus* 4.11, 6.52, 6.53.
14. *Philosophical Investigations* p. 226.
15. Cp. Stewart R. Sutherland, 'On the Idea of a Form of Life' in *Religious Studies,* Vol 11, 1975 and *Atheism and the Rejection of God* pp. 87 ff.

Science Education and Religious Values:

An Islamic Approach

Abdullah Omar Nasseef

Speaking last year at the Institute of Education of London University on the "Role of Faith and Islamic Ethics in the Teaching of Natural and Applied Sciences," I stressed the following points which I would like to restate first before I enter into a discussion of the present topic.[1] I said that the basic consideration of all educational planners is to determine first what education is for and no one can decide that adequately without having a concept of human nature, its growth and development and the purpose of human existence. I also said that the uniqueness of science education cannot be ignored just as we cannot ignore the uniqueness of literary education or education in social sciences. But the uniqueness and the autonomy of various disciplines do not free them from the overall sovereignty of the final aim of education. Claims for the teaching of "pure science" can be entertained only if this teaching does not ignore the inter-relationship of all disciplines and does not make scientists lose the concept of humanity and external nature on which all acquisition and application of knowledge have their deepest impact. The principle of the interrelationship of disciplines is derived from the concept of the total balanced growth of human personality as the aim of education - the aim which was stated at the First World Conference on Muslim Education in the following words: "Education should aim at the balanced growth of the total personality of Man through the training of Man's spirit, intellect, the rational self, feelings and bodily senses. Education should therefore

30

cater for the growth of the human being in all its aspects: spiritual, intellectual, imaginative, physical, scientific, linguistic both individually and collectively and motivate all these aspects towards goodness and the attainment of perfection".[2] The assumptions about human nature that promted this definiton provide the basic framework for the interrelationship of different disciplines. This interrelationship and these assumptions provide an educationist with a method of translating the nature of science and science teaching into educational goals, and of interpreting them in terms of development behavioural descriptions for different educational attainment. I referred to this aspect of science education in general terms in my last lecture. I shall discuss this aspect in greater detail today.

This discussion can become fruitful if we start at first with the religious hypothesis about human nature and its development. As Islam claims to be not a new religion but the final and most complete and comprehensive manifestation of *religion*[3] it asserts the basic concept of human nature which believers in other religions share with the Muslims. Like other religions Islam emphasizes the Supremacy of the Spiritual aspect of human nature which is termed in some religion as its divine aspect or the divinity or Godlines in Man. Islam says that Man can become the Vicegerent of God on earth by cultivating within himself the characteristics that pertain to this Godliness. The attributes of God provide Man with absolute norms of Justice, Knowledge, Charity, Mercy, Love and other qualities. These absolutes can be understood by Man only because he possesses within himself that faculty which helps him to feel and understand the absolutes and become attracted towards it. The more Man cultivates them, the more is he attracted towards them, affected by them and becomes aware of their impact on his whole being. One attribute leads him to another and an internal process is generated that creates within him an aversion to lying, cheating, dishonesty, pride, cruelty, injustice, selfishness, backbiting, and greed and such other habits of man which society has always recognised as "evil". Faith generates within Man the love of God which automatically generates love of the "good" and an aversion to the "bad". It is the spiritual faculty in man that brings about that state of consciousness. Man's rational faculty helps him to justify that consciousness or explain to his own self and to the world at large the need for such experience but it is not the generator of that love. Religious values cannot thus be separated from faith and moral action. As religious experience deepens, faith gets stronger and man becomes more and more conscious both of the ever wider and deeper ranges of objective principles and rules based on the absolutes and of the ever subtler and more comprehensive implications of motives, intentions, feelings, stresses, relationships and circumstances. The life and activities of Prophet Muhammad, peace be on him, provide him with a comprehensive example of the human realisation of the absolutes and thus a human norm to compare himself with, fall back upon and draw upon for personal and communal assessment and for guidance in his own personal choice. It saves him from the freewheeling pluralism that some educators preach without any grain to get hold of. Because of the present-day condition of the twentieth century, it is all the more necessary to teach definite moral values and not deaden the spiritual faculty. If the aim of education is to make man more and more aware of his nature as a human being and his destiny or goal as a vicegerent of God on the Earth so that he may acquire and use his knowledge for creating a world of peace and happiness, it is necessary for him to learn this wisdom given to him by religion.

Does science education contribute at all to this goal or is it entirely neutral or does it make man uncertain, and sceptical about his nature and destiny and therefore turns him into a pragmatical opportunist?[4]

Does science education produce only specialists who are interested only in "pure science" and not in the integral relationship of science education with education as a whole?[5] How far is the attempt since the nineteenth century to establish this relationship governed by the notion that only the philosophy of science based on hypotheses and experiments can provide man with a system of concepts and laws within which science, philosophy and the humanities can fit?[6] However justified from a purist's point of view may be the logical, mathematical and syntactic structure of the physical sciences which are being used as paradigm of the exact or deductive sciences, is it not necessary not to ignore but to understand the constraints on these theories imposed by the metaphysical principles of man and the universe inherent in the religious approach to life and to appreciate the role that these religious-cum-metaphysical principles should have in directing scientific inquiry?[7] In what way and to what extent should the science curriculum in schools be designed to include theories? Have biological and physical sciences experience to offer which can foster intellectual and emotional growth compatible with and sustaining the religious approach to life?[8] Are there concepts or methods of teaching the sciences which reinforce rather than reject the religious attitude to Nature and Life, to physical and biological phenomena, to man's emotional needs, intellectual needs and social needs?

It is obvious that these questions assume the importance of the Spiritual dimension of Man's personality and the individually and socially beneficial aspect of the implicit recognition of the dominance of human spirit and hence of faith and ethical principles based on faith. Because of the historical example of Prophet Muhammad, peace be on him, and the highly emotionally, intellectually and socially beneficial impact of his personality and hence of Islam on the entire world Muslims of the world have never asked for any more justification. As the concept of the good man that

Islam states only reinforces and reestablishes the long-established traditon of humanity to which human nature responds favourably, I do not have to justify here the effectiveness and value of those assumptions. Nor do I intend to lead the discussion into the philosophy of the aims and objectives of education.[9] I have asked the above questions not to generate a discussion about the aims of education but to find out how far education in science fulfil the purpose of education stated earlier.

If the growth of Man as the Vicegerent of God on the Earth is the essence of human existence, if education has to help Man in trying to achieve that end, it is obvious that Man needs knowledge of the world and all creatures and he must understand how he can use this knowledge for the betterment of man, society, the environment and the universe. Science is that branch of knowledge which investigates into the physical and biological world. It is a speculative enterprise. It develops a series of interconnected concepts which result in conceptual schemes that lead man through observation and experimentation into deeper and wider knowledge of physical reality. It is both creative and critical. It is creative in so far as the scientist gets ideas almost intuitively and tries to test his ideas or hypotheses through experiments and observation. At the same time it builds upon existing theories as structure which it does not overthrow without testing its validity from a new premise. The history of science indicates the growth of these ideas and structures through the ages. This development has become accelerated in the last three hundred years and the concept of a mechanistic universe has been replaced by the conccept of an evolutionary world which has got further transformed into a world of relative certainty.[10] Though it may be considered very difficult to establish a school curriculum on theories which may be proved to be false or which may require modification at a later stage, I think it is desirable, more appropriate and truthful to create in students the attitude that all theories may be refutable. This attitude will not create in students an antipathy to the concept of 'creation' and an unfailing devotion to the concept of 'evolution'. The conflict in the scientific attitude to 'natural evolution' and the religious concept of 'creation' by God and manifestation of God's will, power and qualities through this creation was generated in the nineteenth century and is still raging in the world today because of two reasons. The first is the claim of the scientists to have discovered the final truth about the biological origin of species. The second is their claim that *Nature* is an entity having its own laws and it has no awareness of human joy or misery and, as such, there is no direct link between human suffering caused by natural calamity and Man's moral action. The Darwinian attitude was modified by other scientists such as Lamarck. Even then it still remains a problem because the operation of God's Will is denied and nobody asks how *Nature* came into being. The Qur'ān does not deny evolution altogether but it ties up creation with a purpose and separates the creation of one species from the other.[11]

It is this idea of purpose in 'the creation' that the scientists cannot find out by the means employed by them. It is here that the second cause of trouble must be sought. Nature appears to have its own laws but science never considers that Man and his joys and miseries have anything to do with it. Religion teaches us that Man is the master of the universe and that God's attributes of creation, destruction, preservation and maintenance of life - all these are manifested through creation. Modern science does not want to speak of the Will of God or the attributes of God. It avoids discussing the 'creation' of the universe and posits several hypotheses about its origin and operation. Thus the moral principles that religion finds operative in the creation, maintenance, sustenance, growth and the decay of the universe, the principles of love, creation and destruction, justice and injustice, intimately manifested in birth, growth and death of life on this earth are completely ignored by science. But it cannot avoid metaphysics and instead of the religious principles it posits its own ideas. Such a principle is the Darwinian concept of the survival of the fittest - a principle that makes the principle of selfishness and cruelty the operative principle in Nature. Thus the values that religious knowledge teaches pupils as operative in the universe are forgotten or opposed by the education in the sciences. Students come to believe that neither in human nature nor in external nature are there ingrained the basic spiritual principles. There are only certain non-moral physical or biological laws. Similarly they also learn that Nature and human beings are living without any mutual relationship and understanding. Religion teaches us that the universe, in fact the entire creation, is for man and God wants Man to behave as His representative on the Earth. Nature is not a blind force evolving mindlessly in its own way irrespective of whatever may happen to Man and Man must go on having confrontation with Nature. We are also taught that Natural calamities are not just the result of blind forces operating without any idea of what may happen to Man. But they are manifestation of God's warning to Man. Otherwise we shall have to believe that Man is living in a strange world where there is no justice. It is this feeling that science education generates because it eliminates the religious concept. As a result the attitude that is built up is one of enmity and confrontation rather than of love, understanding and justice. It is this attitude that led many governments to ruin environment. Only recently it has dawned on scientists and technologists that destroying natural environment right and left does harm to human beings, that God has set a pattern in this creation which is good for Man. Man has to use it carefully and control and guide it and not ruin it. Scientists and technologists have to learn from religion the purpose of existence and the relationship between external nature and organise their activity accordingly. The authors of the science curricula should develop courses around this central theme of an inherently good relationship between man and Nature. Only from religion can the scientist get the concept of a purpose which he can verify.

The other crucial problem is the control of science. Dickson has very correctly pointed out that "as a result of current educational policy, as well as the organisation and control of scientific activity, science is facing a growing number of problems. These include the increasing number of detrimental effects which scientific and technological developments appear to be having on society; the growing use of science and technology to strengthen the position of economic, industrial or political power elites; the unemployment caused by automation and the introduction of high-capital, rather than labour-intensive technologies; the export to developing countries of technologies totally inappropriate to their economic and social environment; the disproportionate weight of the industrial sector in the selection of priorities in scientific research; and the inability of science to tackle some of the world's most pressing problems such as mass poverty and over-population". (Dickson, D., BSSRS literature, 1971). Dickson suggests that as a remedy three types of consciousness should be integrated into science education: 'Social' consciousness incorporating an awareness of the relationships between science and community; 'environmental' consciousness 'concerned with the impact of sciences on the natural environment and ecological systems', and 'global' consciousness introducing 'an awareness of the problems of world development, the situation faced by the world's under-developed countries, and the part played by science and technology in creating problems!'[12] I agree with Dickson but he forgot the fourth type of consciousness that is central to these three types of consciousness - religious

37

consciousness. The three main topic areas - namely science and the community, science and the environment and science and world development - cannot be developed happily unless the basic attitude required of man towards the community, environment and world as a whole is properly developed. And this can be developed successfully through religious consciousness - a consciousness of man's inherent responsibility towards community, environment and the world as a whole.[13] All these three areas have to be studied concurrently as integrated parts of the science curriculum but religious consciousness alone can instil into these studies an approach to society, environment and the world which is beneficial for mankind. It is from religion that educational planners must learn how the knowledge that science imparts should be organised so that man may acquire power for the benefit and peace and happiness of mankind, how Man can grow up and behave as the Vicegerent of God on Earth.

Whatever I have said implies that though theories formulated by scientists cannot be ignored in framing the science curricula for schools and in programming science research the teaching of theories and planning both the programes and findings of science activity must be subservient to the overall question: how far do they contribute to the fulfilment of the purpose of human existence? This may slow down the speed with which science is progressing. If that is so, let it be. In the last analysis the goal of science teaching and science activity including technology must be a moral goal, as I have stated at the very outset. Where science touches upon peoples lives, values pertain. And no scientist can say that its findings and activities do not touch human life in some form or other. Society cannot be without values and Islam provides mankind with the highest concept of man as God's Vicegerent on the earth. Therefore science education has to be geared to this system and must draw upon such a central scheme of values.

Where there is a confusion of values, scientists will work at cross purposes. The great disparity that we notice today between technological achievement on the one hand and ethical behaviour on the other can only be removed if science education is controlled and directed towards findings and activity ultimately beneficial for mankind and for their environment. Only then can this education help us to strike a balance between intellectual activity and moral progress and we can become fully conscious of the fact that the scientists must not in their absorption with the means, forget the ends and make man forget what all the gadgets are for. Only then can science education become true education.

Notes

1. See *Muslim Education,* Autumn Issue 1982.

2. Recommendation 1.1. in "General Recommendations", See *Conference Book,* King Abdulaziz University, Makkah, Jeddah, 1978 ,p. 78. A similar point of view has been expressed by many thinkers in the West including some religious and some secularist thinkers. Reimer, for example, raises the issue of ideals which are based on value judgements, 'It is not responses that go to schools but individuals who make responses'. He also points out that knowledge is culturally and institutionally controlled. 'But cultures contain ideals'. (Reimer, E., *School is Dead,* Penguin, 1971 pp. 99-102) See also Young, M.F.D. (ed.) *Knowledge and Control,* Collier-Macmillan, 1971.

3. *Religion* is used here not in the Western secular sense according to which it is a form of human consciousness that gradually grew in man and has become outdated. I am using it in the Qur'ānic sense - the sense expressed by the Arabic word *Dīn,* according to which it is an inherent God-consciousness in Man that world and its surroundings make man forget. *Dīn* also means a God-consciousness present in all created objects in the physical and the biological worlds.

4. See Bertrand Rusell's *Impact of Science on Society*, the chapter on "Science and Values".

5. The British Society for Social Responsibility in Science (BSSRS) has already rejected the classical view of pure science as a neutral activity. Science, they say, is a social activity because use of science 'for good or evil by man himself' must be recognised. (BSSRS literature 1969. See also Layton, D. *Trends in Education*, 25, HMSO, 1972, pp. 11-12 'Science', Layton says, 'has now, like classics, to reestablish itself as an effective instrument of general education'. See also *Readings in Science Education*, ed. by Edgar Jenkins and Richard Whitfield, McGraw Hill Book Company (UK) Ltd. 1974, pp. 25-37.

6. For a critical analysis of the historical growth and development of Science-Metaphysics See "Scientific Rationalism" by Giorgio de Santillana in his *Reflections on Man and Ideas*, M.I.T. Press, Cambridge, Mass. U.S.A. & London, England, 1968, pp. 231-270.

7. This point has been discussed by various scientists. An analysis of this point of view of some important scientists is given in James T. Robinson's *The Nature of Science and Science Teaching*, Wadsworth Publishing Co., California, U.S.A., 1968, See pp. 131-137.

8. An attempt to relate purpose of education to the teaching of the sciences has been made in *Disciplines of the Curriculum*, ed. by Whitfield, R.C., Macgraw-Hill, 1971.

9. For a discussion of the aims and objectives of education as seen from the Islamic point of view See: *Aims and Objectives of Islamic Education*, ed. by S.N. al-Attas, Hodder & Stoughton and King Abdulaziz University, 1980. For a ccomparison of these aims with secular aims and their impact on curriculum-making see S.A. Ashraf: *Islamic Curriculum for Muslim Education*, King Abdulaziz University, Jeddah, 1982.

10. Santillana, *op.cit.* pp.231-270.

11. The Qur'ān states that God made stable and firm the earth which was in a liquid form. It also states how before Man was created another species was made of fire called as *jinns* and that there was a time when such a creature as Man was unknown.

12. BSSRS Literature, Dickson, D. 1971.

13. This is typically the Islamic concept on which the entire system of Islamic law *(Sharī'a)* is based. This is known as the rights of People *(ḥuqūq al-'Ibād)*. In addition Islam posits the rights of God *(ḥuqūq-Allāh)*.

Science Education and Religious Values:

A Christian Statement

Paul J. Black

Introduction

This paper attempts to chart the landscape rather than to present a particular argument. In order to do this, it discusses three main areas in three separate sections. The first reviews some of the main issues currently debated in science education itself. A socond section discusses the relationships between science and religion in terms of assumptions about the nature of science and about a Christian perspective on revealed and natural knowledge. The third and final section discusses the main topic, of science and religion in education, in the light of the preceding analysis.

SCIENCE EDUCATION

The aims and scope of science education are subject to searching re-appraisal at present. Fundamental disagreements on this issue marked the first emergence of science as a regular part of the school curriculum a century ago. Layton [1] has described how a struggle developed between a science of common things, in which teaching started from everyday objects, and a high academic science working logically but abstractly from fundamental principles. The latter prevailed and has held sway until recently.

The "high academic science" was always too demanding.

This dilemma was resolved by reducing much of the examining to demands for memorised material. Thus schools and examining authorities cultivated an accommodation between a syllabus with an acceptable number of abstract principles and an examining system that could pass enough of the pupils by requiring rather little understanding of these principles except at the highest grades.

A curriculum reform movement started about twenty-five years ago with the aim of breaking this pattern. It has achieved partial success, in that there has been a shift to emphasising the need for understanding on a narrower range of material. The changes also laid more emphasis on the practical application of scientific principles. However, they reinforced rather than weakened the assumption that the concern of science education with the methods and principles of pure science was its outstanding, almost exclusive, business.

The science curriculum thus retained several features which had been taken for granted by most teachers, whether in schools or universities, for a very long time. The science presented was devoid of philosophical connections - its assumptions were obvious. It was also independent of any considerations of historical or cultural context, apart from snippets of such spurious history as the story of Galileo and the leaning tower of Pisa [2]. Technological and social consequences were largely ignored - the devices that have transformed society were presented for their power to impress pupils with the application of the principles and not in relation to their effects on man's life. Shorn of origins or consequences, the work of scientists was presented as value-free, or rather as a value in itself. The fact that this last lesson was conveyed in default of argument did not diminish its power.

It is now widely accepted that in at least some respects this narrow definition of the arena of science education must be altered. However, this pressure to change is one aspect of a more general upheaveal affecting the science curriculum.

One cause for this upheaval is the need to define a science curriculum appropriate for the average school pupil. The traditional curricula for public examinations were never suitable for more than the top 20% to 30% of the ability range, and attempts to dilute them to serve a much broader range have, by their inadequacy, made the need for a very different approach, more evident. One reason for this has become clearer by research into children's cognitive development and their learning of particular scientific concepts [3,4]. This work shows both that many abstract ideas may have been presented to young pupils at far too early a stage in their development and that pupils have their own robust everyday explanations of much of the evidence which science teaching tries to use to convince them of its principles. These features may lead us back to the need for a science of common things, expecting less in depth of understanding and dealing more with simplified discussion of a wider range of everyday phenomena and artefacts.

A different trend has arisen from those interested in giving more emphasis to the processes of science. Part of the argument for each emphasis is that at least some of these processes will be of direct value to the average citizen after particular facts and concepts have been forgotten. The definition of the processes and their expression in appropriate activities and assessment methods focusses attention on science as a body of methodology, and opens this up to discussion and evaluation [5,6].

The broader approach to the definition of the school science curriculum can be illustrated by the Policy Statement published in 1981 by the Association for Science Education, the professional association of school science teachers in Great Britain [7]. The statement argues that teachers planning and developing the science curriculum "should note that science can be explored from viewpoint of " science as an intellectual dicipline, science as a cultural activity, and science and its applications to work, citizenship, leisure and survival. It goes on to set out six main aims for science education as follows:

"(i) The acquisition of a knowledge and understanding of a range of scientific concepts, generalizations, principles and laws through the systematic study and experience of aspects of the body of knowledge called science.

(ii) The acquisition of a range of cognitive and psycho-motor skills and processes as a result of direct involvement in scientific activities and procedures in the laboratory and the field.

(iii) The utilization of scientific knowledge and processes in the pursuit of further knowledge and deeper understanding, and the development of an ability to function autonomously in an area of science studies to solve practical problems and to communicate that experience to others.

(iv) The attainment of a perspective or way of looking at the world together with some understanding of how it complements and contrasts with other perspectives or ways of organizing knowledge and inquiry.

(v) The attainment of a basic understanding of the nature of advanced technological societies, the interaction between science and society, and the contribution science makes to our cultural heritage.

(vi) The realization that scientific knowledge and experience is of some value in the process of establishing a sense of personal and social identity."

These aims do not reflect present practice, and their implementation will require substantial change.

One set of changes is already directed towards these aims. Two curriculum projects have recently published materials under the titles "Science in Society" and "Science in a Social Context" respectively. Both are designed as optional minority studies for pupils in the sixth form (ages 16-18), this being an area where it is most easy to insert and experiment with the new type of course.

"Science in Society" [8] has main units on health and Medicine, Population, Food and Agriculture, Energy, Mineral Resources, Industry and Economy, Land and Water, Shaping the Future, and Facts. It has been welcomed and used in many schools, but it has also been criticised by some who think it concentrates too much on the industrial economy and takes too many of the values of that economy for granted. "Science in a Social Context" [9] has units entitled: Ways of Living, How Can we be Sure?, Technology, Invention and Industry, Evolution, The Atomic Bomb, Energy, Health, Food and Population, and Space Cosmology and Fantasy. It thus covers a broader range of issues than its rival.

These new course materials are the most tangible evidence of the movement to broaden the definition of the science curriculum. They have their counterparts in higher education - "Science in a Social Context" developed directly from a tertiary sector project of the same name. They serve to underline the main theme of the brief survey in this section - that the nature of science education is now open to debate. Although this debate is hardly concerned at all with religious values, its outcomes may help to establish with pupils and students that the status and effects of the work of science are serious issues with which scientists amongst others must grapple but which science as such cannot resolve.

SCIENCE AND RELIGION

The history of the relations between science and Christianity appears to be a history of conflict. In the famous battles, over Galileo and over Evolution, Christianity was the eventual loser. Religious thought appears to have retreated as a result. Some see the retreat continuing apace as biochemistry, sociobiology and psychology take over the role of understanding who man is and how he lives. Christianity may still fill some churches, but sociology may eventually empty them.

Two results follow from this account in terms of a retreat. Whether or not it be a true and fair one, its hold on many shows that we live with wounds that have never properly healed. It also shows science as the successful invader. In order to develop an understanding of this situation, the discussion below starts by discussing the achievements and assumptions of science before returning to the position of a Christian in reconciling his beliefs with a recognition of the success of science.

Science Successful

The achievements of science are evident. Many scientists feel that these successes follow directly from its reliance on rationality and empirical test. Theories are invented to be sure, but they are tested and abandoned or adapted in the light of evidence. Also, only that knowledge which can be communicated and defended in public, and which can be repeated by others, is allowed to count[10]. The methods and results are open to all, and the community of scientists is an international one, transcending and helping to overcome cultural barriers to understanding and friendship. Above all, the success of science is shown by man's overwhelming success in using its results to conquer nature and to create artefacts which have revolutionised and continue to revolutionise man's life.

47

Whilst much of the above cannot be challenged, it is important to supplement it by drawing attention to several features of the activity of scientists. Firstly, however its activity might be described, science is certainly not a simple recipe of following evidence using organised common sense. Indeed, it can be argued that the achievements which mark the beginning of modern science came about because the mediaeval habit of following the evidence too closely was abandoned in favour of a more bold approach trusting abstractions to guide control of and selection and extrapolation from the evidence to be considered. As Galileo himself put it:

> "Reason hath committed such a rape upon the senses as, in despite thereof to make herself of their credulity." [11]

This theme has been echoed many times since then. Whitehead puts it most clearly:

> "The utmost abstractions are the true weapons with which to control our thought of concrete fact." [12]

and more recent events show the link of abstract theory to technological outcome thus:

> "Ground Control to Apollo 8: "Who is driving up there?"

> Apollo 8 to Ground Control: "I think Isaac Newton is doing most of the driving right now."[13]

Secondly, science is a product of a particular phase of the Christian culture of Western Europe. Whether or not this particular cultural context was essential to its emergence, two beliefs which that context supplied were surely essential to its growth. The first was a belief in the rationality and intelligibility of the natural universe: It is pointless to look for order in events which are controlled by the arbitrary interference of the gods. The second was a belief in the contigent or non-necessary character of the laws of the natural universe. If ideal forms control events, then hard thought will discern their a priori nature and the attempt to refine theory by relentless dialogue with nature's evidence is pointless. This view is set out in Mascall's book[14]: he argues that neither Indian religion nor Greek philosophy could have provided cradle for the growth of science.

The third comment is that the grounds for belief in scientific theories are only remotely empirical. It is rarely the case that a theory of consequence can be falsified by a particular piece of evidence. For the most basic principles, based as they are on their power to make sense of large bodies of evidence, it is hardly possible to imagine evidence that would lead to their downfall. Thus, apparent contradiction of the Principle of Conservation of Energy would have to build up over a long period before any one piece were to lead to more than a reinterpretation of the evidence. Those who study the actual judgements of scientists are now revealing how complex and varied are the factors that determine their choice and use of evidence, and that lead to the neglect of some results and the revolutionary impact of others [15, 16, 17]. Such studies show, amongst other features, the importance of intuition, of criteria, of elegance and simplicity, and of the role of theory in guilding the selection and perception of evidence.

The fourth comment is a special extension of the third. The most general theories of all are those which can hardly be challenged at all without changing the epistemology of science in a fundamental way. These therefore are metaphysical assumptions rather than empirical theories. They include such assumptions as: that the future can be explained in terms of the past, that the whole can be explained solely in terms of the properties of its parts, and that nature is rational and regular but not teleological in its behaviour.

Thus, although it works, science presents its peculiar array of metaphysical and philosophical problems. It is significant that these seem to intensify rather than diminish with the recent progress of science. The shock administered to naive scientists, by the realization that matter refused to behave neatly according to either of their alternative wave or particle models for it, was the first of a series. Indeed, each of the assumptions picked out in the fourth comment is the subject of current debate: the theories of black holes are doing violence to our notion of temporal and causal sequences [18], whilst the complex orchestration of cells has stimulated again debates about both reductionism and teleology in biology [19,20]. Science does not have a simple, explicit and non-problematic method, and it cannot be sure at any one stage that its methods are optimally chosen or even that it is not driving up an expensive blind alley.

Finally, there are quite different considerations from the above which have had a profound impact on scientists. Through their responsibility for the atomic bomb and for some of the ecological disasters and pressures which threaten man's home, scientists now face appalling moral responsibilities. The evasion which separates the responsibility for use from that for invention and development is no longer defensible – if indeed it ever was.

There is however not one, but a spectrum of types of problem. At one extreme, the result of a wholly new experiment may lead to uncontrollable and damaging consequences: the first atomic pile to go critical could have raised such fears had it not been for the secrecy of war. The developing work in genetic engineering has done so, and the scientists in Boston who had to (literally) take a stall in the market place to explain themselves directly to the public in order to secure permission of local politicians for their experiments will have realised their social responsibility in a new way. But cases can differ by many gradations from this extreme, until one reaches a case such as the development of the transistor. That this was done with an eye to new electronic technology is undoubted. However it is hardly possible to imagine that the subsequent development of the social revolution now being caused by the microprocessor could have been weighed in the balance of an argument about whether to proceed with or suppress the work.

Apart from adding the dimension of complex moral choices to the scientist's work, these features also affect the status of scientific activity. That it cannot explain itself easily to the public who are concerned about even allowing it to continue to exist is one problem that may not be seen as fundamental. That it cannot predict all the developments, whether of further scientific principle or of experimental consequence or of technological potential, that may follow from its work is both its glory and its fatal flow.

The scientific method succeeds by limiting sharply the context and conditions for its field of enquiry, often by realising these constraints in artifical "experimental" conditions which in many cases have never occurred in nature. These conditions and the contigent provisional nature of its theories, are both essential to its nature and yet lead inevitably to a lack of control or sure production of consequences. This point is important because if it has been correctly argued, it shows that there is no way to prevent harmful consequences except to suppress science. The risks and the dilemmas are a price that must be paid for engaging in the venture at all.

A Christian Response

The Christian sees his own history and that of the Christain Church as a struggle to discern the deeper meaning of

God's revelation. This revelation is contained both in the world, and in Christ as present through scripture, through the tradition of the Christain Church and through the body of its members. Correctly discerned, this revelation gives access to ultimate explanations of our destiny and that of our universe.

Mistakes have occurred because of a natural tendency to exaggerate the scope or meaning of any one particular part of revelation. By a law analogous to Parkinson's, religious explanation expands to fill the cultural space available, and ultimate explanations are pressed into service to account for the immediate. When expanding secular thought reaches an annexed territory a war many ensure. A priori, it cannot be said that either is the legitimate occupant. But with hindsight, it may be the case that religion has been displaced from a region which it had only occupied by default and not by title.

For example, Galileo's theories were attacked by quoting the incident in the book of Joshua where the sun stood still - if it were perpetually at rest, it was argued, the scriptural account would be in error. Galileo replied that the scripture at this point was to be taken figuratively, not literally, that the scriptures were not given to man to teach him the science of nature and that, since truth cannot conflict with itself, we would do better to pursue the truth in science and be confident that contradictions would turn out to be apparent and not real (see reference 11). These answers did not receive the response they deserved.

The outcome of such lost battles is not without benefit to religion: indeed, if Galileo's third defence could have been taken to heart(by Bishop Wilberforce amongst others) the tension could have been creative. When he "loses" occupied territory, the Christian is forced to look again at the meaning of revelation and can thereby purify his interpretation of it.

The Christian view that has emerged from the tensions

is closely related to a view of God's grace and man's free will. The world belongs to man and he has been given freedom and responsibility to understand and control it. The Christian religion does not provide a way to throw that responsibility back on God, or a set of short cuts to achieve the knowledge and control by which we can realise our destiny. That revelation can guide our ultimate ends and so guide the immediate aims and limits on the work of science is clear, but the boundary between ultimate and immediate is itself an aspect of revelation which we must struggle to discern.

It follows first that there are no cheap or easy ways to resolve the tensions between science and religion. Religion can neither dominate science nor be subject to it. Neither should religious faith use science to "prove" its position, for these "proofs" have to be argued at the metaphysical level, where science is busily engaged in clarifying and justifying its own assumptions. Mascall presents an effective analysis of misguided attempts to show that the "big bang" of scientific cosmology can be "proof" of the Christian belief in God as Creator [14]. The more recent attempts to align modern physics with eastern mysticism seem to commit a similar error [21,22].

Rather must religious faith concede the autonomy of science, and look to profit from interaction with it at all levels, metaphysical, methodological, moral and aesthetic. Enunciated by a Christian living in what is effectively a pluralist and mainly secular state, this position could be misinterpreted as merely a compromise of principle with tactical prudence. However, it is offered here as a statement of principle without compromise. The independence of natural knowledge is a pre-requisite, for the society of freely committed Christians, and for that knowledge to be a genuine and independent contributor to the unfolding of God's revelation of Himself.

SCIENCE AND RELIGION IN EDUCATION

In order to consider the role of science in relation to religion in education, it is first necessary to set out a view of the role and nature of religious education.

One way of locating the role of religious education in the curriculum as a whole is to classify it within one of a set of forms of knowledge or realms of meaning [23,24]. In such a scheme, science might be in one class as the empirical form, whilst religion may be classified as a synoptic form, alongside philosophy and history. However, it might also claim to belong in part to other areas, for example, those concerned with ethics or those concerned with our knowledge and awareness of other persons. The ambiguity that this overlap implies is a symptom of the difficulty of this approach. Religious education is more than a detached appraisal of the beliefs, philosophy, history or sociology of the various world religions.

An approach which tries to analyse and appraise the curriculum in terms of contributions to the needs of the developing child might seem better able to accommodate religious education on its own terms. However, such an approach has to solve the problem of defining what the needs of the child are, or ought to be. Any curriculum policy has to find a way to resolve conflicts between a view of the personal needs of learners and an appraisal, in terms of priorities and of balance, of the attitudes, values, knowledge and skills that can be taught. Within such a resolution, the specific function of religious education must be to offer ways to confront and work on questions of ultimate commitment, in belief, in personal and social relationships and in morality.

This enterprise has to work with both experience and intellect. The mystery of how man is capable of knowing, loving and creating is one which all can approach first through reflection on their experience and few can approach from any a priori rational analysis. By whatever route, the eventual aim is to provoke interplay between thought, feeling and motivation.

O'Leary and Sallnow [25] argue that such an approach in no way devalues scripture and doctrine:

> "The function of explicitly religious content therefore is to illuminate and bring to a full level of awareness in the child the full meaning and value of his experiences."

Religious education also has to choose a route between two extremes. One is that of the teaching, by committed believers, of ideas that can allow of no challenge, the other that of the detached study by agnostics. The former can stunt maturity by indoctrination, the latter can be equally debilitating by treating commitment externally, as a problem that other people have.

In our society, any approach by indoctrination is bound to fail. We know that the product of indoctrination is too often fragile. It tends to produce firm commitment only in those whose immaturity prevents them exercising their full freedom of choice. The Christian teacher of religion has had to learn to walk a tight-rope between honest and full expression of his own commitment and respect for the need of his pupils to progress as carefully and as freely as possible to making their own commitments in their own way. The pursuit of this delicate equilibrium has become an end in itself, in that, although it may have been adopted through necessity, it is embraced now as a more valid ideal than that of narrow indoctrination.

Rather similar arguments arise if claims are made that religion should be a centralising or unifying force across the whole of education. The particular Christian view I present here is that religion cannot rule other areas of man's search for understanding. Each requires a free relation of the knower to the known, which can be prejudiced by imposing restraints from outside, whether from religion or from elsewhere. One must believe that such restraints would ultimately impoverish if one believes that grace acts through nature.

This need for autonomy is not in conflict with a need to reconcile and unify the various sources of our understanding. Progress in natural knowledge could hardly advance our understanding of a church's traditions or of scriptural revelation if the effort to interrelate and unify were not continually being made. However the independence of the contributors is a condition for the authenticity of this particular debate, and it guarantees that it will be renewed over time.

SCIENCE AND RELIGIOUS EDUCATION

If religious education's role were to be seen in the way outlined above, then the various developments in science education described in my opening section could be considered in relationship to it. In so far as science education moves towards accepting argument over the social, epistemological and moral implications as part of its remit, it is presenting science as an input with which the more fundamental questionings of religion can engage.

To achieve such a shift will take considerable effort. It is well known that it is difficult, whether in universities or in schools, to break down barriers between subject departments. So, little may be achieved unless, within their barriers, science teachers are ready to broaden their approach and so find something in common with teachers of religion, whose efforts to broaden may include greater attention to science as a part of man's experience.

However, the traditional courses for degree education in university science are so narrow in scope that any linking to religion, or even to any other intellectual discipline, can seem an irrelevant intrusion. Such courses produce graduates for secondary science teaching who lack preparation, both in intellect and in attitude, for teaching science in a broader way. In addition, such teaching calls for a style of interaction with pupils which is foreign to many scientists: I have heard teachers declare that it would not be possible to teach or examine on matters of opinion — overlooking the fact that many of their colleagues in other areas do this most of the time. Recognition of these difficulties could impose modesty on any programme for change, but need not prevent an exploration of its nature and purpose.

The need outlined here is not for science teachers to become more religious or to pay particular attention or lip-service to religion in their teaching. The plea rather is that they become more concerned with broadening the contribution that their work makes to the total education of pupils and students. They should emphasise more the power of man's knowledge and the paradox that this goes with uncertainty about the nature of the enterprise and about the rules by which it progresses. They should point to the technological consequences which have enriched mankind's life, threatened it in the most fearful ways, and moved scientists from the witness box to the dock when humanity puts on trial those who threaten it. They should point to man's sense of the wonders and complexity of the universe, which scientific study deepens and enhances rather than explains away. To quote a theoretical physicist, Paul Davies, at the conclusion of his book *The Forces of Nature:*

> "No-one who has studied the forces of nature can doubt that the world about us is a manifestation of something very very clever indeed."[26]

All of this is a plea that science education should have, in human terms, more light and shade, more significance and more problems, more humanity and less mechanism. It must escape from the grey pallor that pervades much of the taken-for-granted and culture free science that is currently taught.

If he has such an approach, the science educator begins to labour in a vineyard next door to his religious colleagues. They can start to speak over the wall and exchange materials and appraoches. But neither must try to annex all of the other's land. Both must try to serve the same end which is the full development of the pupils whom they both teach.

Herein lies a final problem. Our education cannot work to some grand synthesis of knowledge when, in our culture, such a synthesis does not exist. Whether or not it could or should, each individual has to make and constantly revise his own combination, and grapple with the inconsistencies that arise. Many of us cannot do this for ourselves, or have decided to live with our own evasions of the task. This fact may explain why the labour devoted to delivering the various specialist areas to our learners stands in contrast to the neglect of the task of helping them to see them in relation to one another and to their own personal needs. It may explain, but it may not excuse.

Notes

1. Layton, D., *Science for the People,* George Allen and Unwin, London 1973.
2. Cooper, Lane, *Aristotle, Galileo and the Tower of Pisa,* Cornell University Press, Ithaca, N.Y. 1935.
3. Shayer, M. and Adey, P., *Towards a Science of Science Teaching,* Heinemann, London 1981.
4. Driver, Rosalind, *The Pupil as Scientist,* Open University Press, Milton Keynes 1983.
5. Harlen, W., Black, P. and Johnson, S., *Science in Schools Age 11 Report No. 1,* Her Majesty's Stationery Office, London 1981.
6. Schofield, B. et al. *Science in Schools Age 13 Report No. 1,* Her Majesty's Stationery Office, London 1982.

7. Association for Science Education, *Education Through Science — Policy Statement,* A.S.E., Hatfield, Herts. 1981.
8. Lewis, J.L., *Science in Society — Teacher's Guide,* Heinemann, London and A.S.E. Hatfield 1981.
9. Addinell, Sue and Solomon, Joan, *Science in a Social Context,* A.S.E. Hatfield, Herts. 1983
10. Ziman, J., *Public Knowledge,* Cambridge University Press, London 1968.
11. de Santillana, *The Crime of Galileo,* Mercury Books, Heinemann, London 1961.
12. Whitehead, A.N., *Science in the Modern World,* New York, Macmillan 1931.
13. Quoted in J.L. Lewis, op. cit. p.162.
14. Mascall, E.M., *Christian Theology and Natural Science,* Longmans, London 1956.
15. Polanyi, M., *Personal Knowledge,* Routledge and Kegan Paul, London 1958.
16. Lynch, M.E., "Technical Work and Scientific Enquiry: Investigations in a Scientific Laboratory", *Social Studies of Science* 12 (4) 499-533, 1982.
17. Stokes, T.P., "The Double Helix and the Worped Zipper: An Exemplary Tale", *Social Studies of Sciences* 12 (2) 207-240, 1982.
18. Davies, Paul, *The Runaway Universe,* J.M. Dent, London 1978.
19. Monod, Jacques, *Chance and Necessity,* W. Collins, Glasgow 1972.
20. Peacocke, A.R. *Creation and the World of Science,* Clarendon Press, Oxford 1979.
21. Restivo, S., "Parallels and Paradoxes in Modern Physics and Eastern Mysticism", *Social Studies of Science* Vol. 12 (1), 37-71, 1982.
22. Peacocke, A. R., op. cit. p.360.
23. Phenix, P., *Realms of Meaning* McGraw Hill, New York 1964.
24. Hirst, P., *Knowledge and the Curriculum,* Routledge and Kegan Paul, London 1966.
25. O'Leary, D.J. and Sallnow, T., *Love and Meaning in Religious Education,* Oxford University Press, Oxford 1982.
26. Davies, P., *The Forces of Nature,* Cambridge University Press 1979.

Literary Education And Religious Values:

An Islamic Approach

Syed Ali Ashraf

The relationship between literary education and religious values can be properly appreciated only after we ascertain the necessity, range and depth of the religious basis for education, formulate the aims and objectives of education with reference to that basis and assess the nature, quality and depth of the contribution that literary education makes towards the realization of those aims and objectives. The nature of this relationship becomes clearer when the nature of literature is explored and the syllabi and the content of literary courses and their teaching methodology are examined and ascertained with reference to those aims and objectives. A preliminary investigation into some aspects of this topic was made by me in 1977 reference to which will be made in due course[1].

As regards the aims and objectives of education and its religious basis, the Islamic approach has been discussed in the four world conferences on Muslim education, in the books in the *Islamic Education Series* and other subsequent publications on education by King Abdul Aziz University. So far as the Muslim States are concerned, they have, through their Makkah Declaration made at the third meeting of the Head of the States held in 1981, theoretically accepted the ideal stated in the definition of education and its aims enunciated at the First World Conferences on Muslim Education held in Makkah al-Mukarramah in 1977. When we analyse the range and depth of this definition and understand its basis we realise that the definition is surely directed towards entire humanity and not merely towards the Muslims but its implementation may vary according to the interpretation that may be given and the value-content that may be imagined by particular communities or groups of people.

The definition is as follows: "Education should aim at the balanced growth of the total personality of Man through the training of Man's spirit, intellect, the rational self, feelings and bodily senses. Education should therefore cater for the growth of the human being in all its aspects: spiritual, intellectual, imaginative, physical, scientific, linguistic, both individually and collectively and motivate all these aspects towards goodness and the attainment of perfection."[2] It goes on further to explain the purpose of this growth and says that "the ultimate aim of Muslim education lies in the realization of complete submission to Allah on the level of the individual, the community and humanity at large".[3] By "Muslim education" one obvious meaning implied is the education of the community that is generally known as "Muslims". The other meaning of this phrase is in implications of the word "Muslim" which means a person who submits his will to God's Will. For such a person education is a process through which he can grow up as a faithful, pious and righteous individual, a means to learn how to acquire knowledge in all its branches and how to use it for the benefit of mankind. For him it is a method which helps his innate faculties to develop in a balanced way when he uses knowledge for 'good' purpose and thus he gets pleasure through the development of certitude and his understanding of God's ways in the universe. He thus draws nearer and nearer to God and becomes, at last, if he has that highest innate potentiality, a true representative of God on Earth, *Khalīfatullāh*, vicegerent of God on Earth. [4]

Religion thus provides education with a concept of man which is undoubtedly the richest and noblest concept of

man as the representative of God on Earth. Prophet
Muhammad, peace be on him, asked his followers to
cultivate the characteristics of God. By characteristics are
meant the attributes of God which are expressed through
the Names of God. "Call upon God," the Qur'ān says, "or
call upon the God of Mercy by whichever you will invoke
Him. He hath most excellent and Beautiful Names."[5] The
first educated man according to the Qur'ān was Adam
whom God taught the Names or everything. Names thus
signify the essence of everything and the essence thus
manifests the qualities of God which are absolute. The
Qur'ān thus tells us that Man is potentially the inheritor of
these attributes and by cultivating them he acquires that
wisdom which helps him to serve God as His true representative. To invoke God by His Names means to acquire
those characteristics by keeping that absolute Norm in
front of Man. It further implies the breaking down of
barriers that contingent circumstances impose on Man's
Self - the barriers that blind his eyes and deafen his ears and
make him narrow and selfish be that the narrowness of
himself, his family, race, colour or creed. Thus, by "invoking
the Names" he learns to expand his self, to sympathise, to
effect a real catharsis of his emotions. It is this expansion
and transformation of the human Self or the "contingent"
and subjective self into the 'absolute' 'universal' and
objective Self that is referred to in the following statement
of the Prophet. He said, "God says, my slave seeketh
unremittingly to draw nigh unto Me with devotions of his
free will until I love him, and when I love him, I am the
hearing wherewith he heareth and the sight wherewith he
seeth, and the hand wherewith he smiteth and the foot
whereon he walketh".[6]

Religion provides education not only with the norm of
ideal values but also the means of reaching them. It gives
man certitude that faith brings, faith in God and faith in the
existence of his Spirit, the Spirit breathed into him from

God's own spirit. It is this infinity and eternity within him that enables him to comprehend the Infinity and Eternity of God.

The same is true of the method. Religion teaches us that Love is the only method of achieving complete realization. Love implies a merging of the one into the other, however separate their existence may be. Education therefore does not mean merely an intellectual acquisition of some ideas and concepts or some factual knowledge of external reality. It means a process that transforms one's attitude to life and generates within the individual a hankering for the ideal. Hankering implies the want of the thing hankered for. It also implies a latent knowledge which man bears unconsciously and 'eternally' within him which religion awakens through love for the Prophet who historically personifies the ideal and symbolises the human goal. This method of realizing Truth is prescribed by religion because it is the only possible mode of man's participation in the divine truths. The "rational mode of knowledge", as Frithjof Schuon rightly points out, "in no way extends beyond the realm of generalities and cannot by itself reach any transcendent truth ...... When philosophy uses reason to resolve a doubt, this proves precisely that its starting point is a doubt which it is striving to overcome, whereas the starting point of a metaphysical formulation is always essentially something intellectually evident, or certain."[7] The spiritual organ which the Muslims call 'the eye of the heart' takes man beyond the mundane realm of 'proofs' and ordinary 'beliefs' into the region of absolute certainty. Love opens that eye because love of the Prophet generates automatically love for truths. It is this participatory role that transforms individual and collective personality through continuous and increasing assimilation of values.

This participation become a source of immense pleasure mainly because it is a result of personal choice. Man has got the freedom to accept or reject this role. The inner dimension of knowledge can never be realized without a decision of the Will to actively follow the process that the tradition of the prophets has laid down for our convenience. A large number of people today are afraid of realizing those values fully in their individual and collective life because of their lack of understanding, because they have been taught to start with doubts and not with love for the ritual, because of the confusion of educators between generalities and transcendent truths. There is too much stress on individual realization and hardly any assertion of universal, transcendent value-criteria to assess the truth or fasity of individual response to truth.

It is here that literary education can make a positive contribution. Literature is a branch of knowledge. Though God is all-knowing and therefore all knowledge belongs to Him, one form of knowledge is directly revealed by God without Man's efforts. This is "Revealed Knowledge" given to man through the prophets and, according to the Qur'ān, in its final perfected and complete form through Prophet Muhammad, peace be on him. All other forms of knowledge need, on the part of man, efforts with a particular goal in view, that was why at the First World Conference on Muslim Education all the other branches were placed in the category of "Acquired Knowledge". Literature is one of the branches of "Acquired Knowledge".

Literature, however, is different from other branches of acquired knowledge such as natural sciences and social sciences, and more akin to revealed knowledge in its mode of acquiring knowledge and in its manner of presentation. A scientist starts with a hypothesis and tries to find out how far it is true. From the data collected by him he generalises and establishes his conclusions. Karl Popper speaks of inspiration as the source of hypothesis. However true that may be the mode of establishing the truth of that hypothesis is doubt, data collections, argumentation, attempt to refute that hypothesis and modification, refutation or establishment of truth. Social sciences follow a similar pattern and they establish their conclusions by pure induction. Literature depends mainly on the intuitive realisation of some truths about life which the imagination of the author seizes and turns into a poem or a novel or a drama. This realisation is similar to a revelation received by a prophet in both being universal and transcendent. They both transcend the limitations of time and space. But whereas literary truth is circumscribed by the limitation of individual experience, insight and ability, prophetic revelation is free from such limitations because it expresses what God wants to reveal through the prophet, not what the prophet wants to know. The condition of their realisation of truth is also similar. A prophet submits his will to God's Will by banishing from his mind all matters of self-interest, and thus by making his whole attitude to life selfless, 'disinterested' and untrammelled by personal prejudices so that truth could be reflected within himself and the principles of justice, mercy and righteousness can become operative through him. This was what was known as purification (*tazkiyah* in Arabic). A prophet was of course doing this consciously through fasting, prayer and remembrance of God. From the history of traditional writers and artists we know that they also believed that they should get the reflection of ultimate reality only if they purify themselves and quite often they would also take recourse to fasting and prayer. Those writers of today who do not believe in God or in any particular religion also purify themselves in some form or other and that is what Coleridge calls "detachment" and Matthew Arnold "disinterestedness". Ananda Coomaraswamy explains this as the subjection of the artist's "sensitive psychophysical Ego to the spiritual or intellectual self".[9] Whereas the traditional writer or artist would regard this "whole process" (of preparation) as one "of worship"[10], the modern writer regards it as an attempt to clear the intense inner focus of irrelevances. Whether

65

the writer is conscious of God or not, the purpose is the same - an attempt to transcend the limitations of the outward self, the limitations imposed upon the spirit or veiling the eyes of the spirit by the experience of our day to day external existence and hence by passions and sense-perceptions. If the writer does not cross this realm of sensation and desires and reach that stage of consciousness which helps him to be objective in his vision, he cannot understand the actual status of sensations and desires in his whole range of realisations.

It is only when a writer reaches that stage that the contemplative or intellectual phase of the creative process can begin. The poet thus proceeds from the sensation that physical beauty rouses to the contemplation of Beauty in the world. "Every beauty", says Ghazzali , "in the world is a spark of the permanent Beauty of God and a spark of High light. So can he not love Him who is ever beautiful and the prime source of beauty?"[11] The same idea is expressed in Scholastic terminology in the following words: "The whole purpose of contemplation .... is to reach that state of being in which there is no longer any distinction of Knower from Known, or being from Knowing".[12] That is the state when the poet says to the nightingale, "Already with thee"[13] or like Wordsworth feels Nature along the pulse but goes beyond it and hears

> "truths that wake,
> To perish never"

and their souls "have sight of that immortal sea".[14] It is to this experience and realization that Keats referred to when he said that Wordsworth had gone into the fifth chamber of the mind whereas he was still lingering in the first chamber.[15]

This certitude is possible according to Plato whenever the creator (writer or artificer) "looks to the unchangeable and fashions the form and nature of his work after an unchangeable pattern ... but when he looks to the created only, and uses a created pattern, it is not fair "perfect".[16] Plotinus explains this stage of consciousness and the relationship between the writer and the image of truth that comes to him in the following words: "In contemplative vision, especially when it is vivid, we are not aware of our personality; we are in possession of ourselves, but the activity is towards the object of vision with which the speaker becomes identified; he has made himself over as matter to be shaped; he takes ideal form under the action of the vision, while remaining potentially himself." [17]

It is but obvious that as the poet is seeking something permanent, he cannot find it in external world because it is continually changing, only its essence is permanent. In Islamic metaphysics, Ibn 'Arabi explains this work of creative imagination as the search for and the realization of *'ālam al–mithāl* (the world of Idea-Images) a world between the world of spiritual realities and the sensible world - an intermediary world which culminates in the notion of the symbol.[18]

The poet thus is not just reorganizing his/her sense-experience and presenting them to the reader, he is allowing his spirit to penetrate to the innermost meaning of his experience with the help of the insight that the absolute within him bestows him with. That is what Eckhart meant when he said "Let go thyself and let God act for thee"[19] which Coomaraswamy explains by saying, "The arising of the image is not by an act of will .. but of attention ... when the will is at rest".[20] And this is why Blake said, "one Power alone makes a Poet: Imagination, the Divine Vision".[21] That is why Keats asks Fancy to let herself "loose" and discover eternal Beauty [22] and Dylan Thomas boasts that "death shall have no dominion".[23] Coleridge explains this as the power of imagination which he conceives as a faculty whose action is "the repetition in the finite mind of the eternal act of creation in the infinite I AM." [24]

This search for something eternal and permanent,

something universal and transcendent is true both of literature that deals with external nature and literature that deals with human life. The main intention of the author is not to depict nature just as it is externally or depict human life as it is seen in actual life because both are externally impermanent and changeable. Human society seems to change more rapidly and drastically today and it is becoming more and more difficult for the authors to find the permanent principle of existence and a suitable image that would manifest this principle. The intention is to use an image as a symbol of eternity and perfection and a norm of human nature with the help of which the author may represent the truth he has discovered.

In the twentieth century, as Auden points out, it has become extremely difficult for the author to discover these attributes or qualities in external or human nature and present them through images and situations that would convey that feeling. Auden says that nowadays there is a 'loss of belief in the eternity of the physical universe' because modern science gives us a picture of nature as a process in which nothing is now what it was or what it will be. Science has made it difficult for a modern artist to believe he can make an enduring object when he has no model of endurance to go by ; he is more content than his predecessors to abandon the search for perfection as a waste of time and be content with sketches and 'improvisations'.[25] Auden further points out that there was a time when men believed the sensory phenomena were the invisible sign of the inward and invisible, 'but both were believed to be real and visible,' but as modern science has destroyed our faith in this naive observation of the senses 'authors can no longer consider a nature "out there" be truly or falsely imitated'.[26] But the greatest blow is the loss of belief in a 'norm of human nature which will always require the same kind of man-fabricated world to be at home in.' [27] As a result the author cannot depend on the traditional norm. He has to create his own norm afresh out of his own experience and observations. The question then arises: if the condition of the literary world is as Auden describes, how far can literary education contribute to the fulfilment of the objectives stated in the definition of education given at the First World Conference?

In order to answer this question it is necessary for us to keep in view the following two things: firstly, the difference and similarities between religion and literature which has been pointed out earlier resulting in the difference in the methodologies of imparting religious education and literary education and, secondly, the methods adopted by writers to overcome the difficulties stated by Auden in order to convey their hankering for or realization of something permanent or eternal, in other words, some attributes of God, in some form or other, and the impact of this on the teaching method.

As regards the former it has already been stated that religion directly calls man to God and gives him a code of life which would prepare him physically, mentally, spiritually and socially to draw him closer to God by cultivating within him those values whose roots are in the attributes of God and which God has planted within him as potentialities. Literature (except devotional literature whose purpose ultimately is the same as above) intends to convey to him through images drawn from his life (including his environment) individual realization of some truths which, the writer feels, transcends local, temporal, changeable reality. Because religious values are part and parcel of the whole code of life granted to Man by God, they are to be taught directly as transcendent and universal and as belonging to a whole. Literature, being the product of individual realization, cannot have that completeness of a code of life and must be read and taught as the individual intuitive realization of the same Truth and, hence, as being incomplete and partial, however transcendent and universal that realization may be.

This aspect of literature may be appreciated only at the last stage of teaching literature which I would like to call the 'evaluatory' stage. The primary stage of understanding is the stage of the appreciation of language, rhythm and form. Form includes the whole structure of the poem or the narrative or the drama. As students go on analysing and reintegrating the meaning of language, rhythm and structure and thus understanding the meaning of the form they go on responding with their feeling to the work of art. As arousing of feelings is the means of carrying the reader into the world of reality intuitively realized by the author, students must be taught to distinguish between false, banal and true feelings. Here it is necessary for the teacher and the taught to have a full awareness of the literary tradition so that students may assess the use of language and rhythm and are not carried away by cliché and sentimentality. It is also at this stage that the evaluation of the range and depth of the universality and transcendence of truth expressed in literature begins. The norm of religious experience described earlier provides a norm for the evaluation of this experience enshrined in literature. This norm cannot be imposed but it provides a ready reference provided the teacher who would teach the process of evaluation has got the intellectual intuition necessary for such an experience. As a matter of fact when the response to literature rouses the feelings and the reader is compelled to get out of his narrow world into a new world of experience and a contemplative consciousness is induced, his inquisitive and responsive spirit starts an intuitive evaluation provided he has the intellectual cognition and certitude about the basic norm. If he does not possess the insight that comes from certitude it is better for him to stop after analysing the nature, and quality of his own response. A person who possesses that intuitive certainty can ignite the soul of others by his own response and analysis. He understands how far the writer has succeeded in conveying the sense of probability. All writings in this sense are symbols of reality. By creating the sense of probability the symbol succeeds in moving the heart and in conveying the Truth about life.

It is this symbolic nature of literature that takes us to the second point that has been mentioned earlier - the methods adopted by a twentieth century writer when he finds that there is a breakdown of communications for want of a commonly accepted norm of good and evil. As he finds that it would be difficult for him to create a sense of probability if he assumes the traditional value-norm which is based on religion, he starts creating symbols or seeks and reasserts those archetypal symbols which traditional literature had always taken resort to or go back to old myths and give new meaning to them. In order to understand the real meaning of these figures of thought that are not merely figures of speech it is necessary for the teacher to make extensive study of many literatures in which the meanings of symbols are explained and must himself learn to think in those terms. As Coomaraswamy puts it, "it is in this universal, and universally intelligible language that the highest truths have been expressed."[28] Symbols and myths become a means of rescue when there is a decline in our divinity and spirituality. This is the reason for which great writers like Yeats, Eliot and Kafka create new myths or give new meaning to traditional myths in order to delineate the pattern of human and cosmic events as realised by them.

It is therefore the duty of the teacher of literature not to insist on aesthetic pleasure as the aim of reading literature. Aesthetic pleasure is only a means to lull the argumentative self asleep and lead the reader into the stage of the contemplation of Reality presented by the writer. Literary education thus is complementary to religious education.

It is here that the teacher has to play a vital role. Writers

71

today may often theorise and formulate a philosophy of their own. It is necessary for the teacher to indicate how the writer has strayed beyond the experience, how values evolved by the writer are highly occult, personal and dogmatic and how the writer is using literature as a means of conveying a philosophy and a way of life which is not the direct outcome of moral or spiritual experience. "When a writer tries to propagate a philosophy he should be criticised from the extra-literary point of view, which is the point of view of a thinker".[29]

Whereas previously I had said that it is the teachers' job to teach students how to respond correctly to the Truths presented by the author, now I would like to indicate his role as a mentor and guide so that he may indicate the limitations of the work in hand and point out "how far the writer's emotive response to the human situation is governed by his day to day convention and customs, and how far the writer has succeeded in concentrating his attention on essential, universal human problems which are surrounded by socio-cultural accretions or which have their particular slant and complexity because of contemporary socio-cultural conditions".[30]

The teacher can do so only when he himself has imbibed a norm of life. From the Islamic point of view religion gives him the noblest concept of humanity and shows him the way of life that enables man to reach the zenith of greatness, and also the other way that leads to self-destruction, a norm that provides him with criteria about right and wrong, good and evil. If a teacher imbibes that norm he will be able to measure the extent of a writer's response to life, his range, variety and his individual typical way of responding to human situations. As different writer's responses are bound to be different, the teacher can choose a variety of literary works for study. Students then can see the variety of perceptions and the variety of effects. This will enable students to compare and evaluate the particular varieties of truths enshrined in different literary works. The complete code of life that religion provides enables a student to understand the shortcomings, limitations and greatness of literary effects with reference to a complete norm of existence. It is about this aspect of teaching that I had said, "The teacher's function ... is not to settle all morally critical questions in advance. He has to make a selection of works which will provide apt contrasts in moral sensibilities and ensure free and frank discussion on the sensibilities they embody".[31]

I would here like to end with a quotation from what I said five years ago about the relationship between literary education and ethical education.

"If by aesthetic education is meant the development of the ability to perceive fully and understand adequately the beautiful and its meaning in the arts, it needs to be complemented by ethical education so that the relationship between the good and the beautiful is felt and appreciated. This is only possible when the beautiful is understood to be a manifestation of the great principle of Beauty, which is nothing less than an attribute of God. The variations in aesthetic judgements are the results of the different emphases that are placed on different aspects of human personality in different ages .... Otherwise man is eternally and universally the same creature.

"In order that aesthetic education may become part and parcel of the education of the total personality of Man it is necessary to strike a balance between spiritual, rational and aesthetic perceptions. We will create a disintegrated personality if we assert that there is such a thing as 'pure sensation' or 'pure thinking' or 'pure aesthetic' perception. As Truth and Beauty are the attributes of God and as this entire creation is nothing but the manifestation of all the Qualities and Powers of God, or, in other words, the attributes of God, the reflection in art of this Beauty and Truth is nothing but a reflection of the beautiful in life.

Thus aesthetics connects the teaching of the beautiful in the arts with the teaching of ethics."[32]

Notes

1. "Islamic Principles and Methods of Teaching Literature" by Syed Ali Ashraf in *Philosophy, Literature and Fine Arts,* ed. by Seyyed Hossein Nasr, Hodder & Stoughton & King Abdulaziz University, London, 1982, pp. 22-48.
2. "Recommendation1.1" in *Conference Book,* King Abdulaziz University, Jeddah, 1978, p. 78.
3. *ibid,* p. 78.
4. As stated in the Qur'ān, "Behold, thy Lord said to the angels: I will create a vicegerent on earth", II: 30.
5. *Qur'ān,* XVII: 110.
6. *Hadīth Qudsi.*
7. *The Transcendent Unity of Religions,* by Frithjof Schuon, Faber & Faber, London, 1953, pp. 11-12.
8. See *Conference Book,* op cit, pp. 78-79.
9. 'Athena and Hephaistas' in *Journal of Indian Society of Oriental Art,* Vol XV.
10. *Figures of Speech or Figures of Thought,* by Ananda Coomaraswamy, London, 1946, p. 151.
11. See Ghazzali's *Ihyā' 'Ulūm al-Dīn* translated by Fazlul Karim, Dhaka, 1971, p. 211.
12. *Figures of Speech or Figures of Thought,* op cit, p. 151.
13. 'Ode to a Nightingale'.
14. 'Ode on the Intimations of Immortality'.
15. Keats' Letters .
16. *Timaeus,* 28A, B Jowett's translations.
17. *Enneads,* IV, 4, 2.
18. *Creative Imagination in the Sufism of Ibn Arabi* by Henry Corbin, Tr. Ralph Mannheim, Routledge & Kegan Paul, London, 1969, p. 217. See the whole chapter IV, on 'The Ophanic Imagination and Creativity of Heart', pp. 216–245
19. Eckhart I, 18–19.
20. *The Transformation of Nature in Art,* Cambridge, Mass. 1935, p. 76.
21. *Poetry and Prose of William Blake* by Geoffrey Keynes (ed), London, 1948, p. 821.

22.   "Fancy" by Keats.

23.   "Death shall have no dominion" by Dylan Thomas.

24.   *Biographia Literaria* by Coleridge, OUP, 1907, p. 202.

25.   "The Poet & the City" in *The Dyer's Hand and Other Essays* by H. Auden, Vintage Books Edition, USA, 1968, p. 78.

26.   *ibid*, p. 78.

27.   *ibid*, p. 79.

28.   *Figures of Speech or Figures of Thought,* op cit, p. 122.

29.   "Islamic Principles and Methods in the Teaching of Literature" by S. A. Ashraf, op cit, p. 29.

30.   *ibid*, p. 31.

31.   *ibid*, p. 37.

32.   *ibid*, pp. 39-40.

Literary Education And Religious Values:
A Christian Approach

Stephen Medcalf

In this country the question "Are you a Christian?" may be received either with the kind of embarrassment which shows that the intent of the words is as it would have been in my boyhood - "Do you try to love God and man seriously?" - or else, what became really common only in the sixties, with the "yes" or "no" which assumes that the questioner is distinguishing the moral and intellectual pattern of a Christian from those of a Muslim, a Jew, a Hindu, an atheist or an agnostic.

The first interpretation is appropriate to a country whose basic structures (language, pattern of the year, state rituals, law, literature, townscape) are deeply informed by Christianity. In such a country, a Christian is tempted by two presuppositions about values and intellectual approaches: first that there are so many such various Christian approaches that it is foolish to look for any common Christian factor; secondly, that all possible approaches, whether derived from Christianity or not, are more or less reconcilable with it. The Lord said, "He who is not against me is for me."

The second interpretation is appropriate to a country hospitable to all faiths, a free country informed by liberalism, where it is recognised not only that many faiths exist within the national boundaries, but also that agnosticism and atheism are themselves faiths, and not simply failings to take Christianity, or any other religion, seriously. In such a country, a Christian may be tempted to feel, either that all values and intellectual approaches which fall outside the sphere of the religious, whatever that is, are likely to be tainted with corruption, to be a threat to Christianity (the Lord also said: "He who is not with me is against me."): or else that such values and approaches being merely secular, not in themselves friendly or hostile to Christianity, may be followed freely. But I suspect that this last indifferentism, common as it is, is not really reconcilable with a religion that holds itself relevant to the whole of experience.

In fact, however, since it is uncertain which interpretation the question is likely to bear, there is an ambiguity about how to respond, and indeed often enough an embarrassingly ambiguous response. A Christian in England as it is now, is singularly blessed in that, while he is sustained by the basically Christian structures which I have mentioned, he can readily stand outside the limiting presumptions which follow from them: can see, for example, that values which he and some of the agnostics among his friends take for granted are in fact oddly religious. He cannot (or cannot without careful thought) take any of the simple positions so far mentioned, but must return to the fundamental Christian and Biblical beliefs which govern any possible Christian understanding of values and intellectual approaches, and hence of literature and education.

There are perhaps seven such beliefs, of which the first five concern creation and incarnation:

First, that in the beginning God created the world by His Word, and saw that it was good.

Secondly, that God created man in His own image, and as His vicegerent in the world.

Thirdly, that the Word by which God created the world is the word - inner light, reason, consciousness - that lightens every man coming into the world.

Fourthly, that the Word was made flesh, and the glory of God revealed in Jesus.

These four are all from the beginnings of *Genesis* and of the Gospel of John.

Fifthly, from the Athanasian Creed, that the Word was made flesh, not by conversion of the Godhead into flesh, but by taking of the manhood into God. This may seem more abstruse than the first four doctrines: but it has large implications, directly for the destiny of mankind in relation to God, that is the unity of mankind at large with God (the deification, it has been called, of man), and by analogy for the relation of symbol to meaning, as we shall see later.

It is entirely congruous with these first five doctrines that all Christians always have believed that there are words that form a literature composed by men enlightened by the Word of God, glorifying the world, interpreting the world, and bringing the attention of men through the world to God, which literature it is a part of Christian life to study. One of the fathers of English literature, Bede, expresses this belief in his prayer:

"I pray you, good Jesus, that as you have given me the grace to drink in with joy the word that gives knowledge of you, so in your goodness you will grant me to come at length to yourself, the source of all wisdom, to stand before your face for ever."

So far as the five beliefs which I have outlined go, this Word might be co-extensive with all literature, indeed with everything that any man ever writes or says. This might, I suppose, be true in Paradise, and the most paradisal Christian thinker known to me says that it is true of this world, if we take the right way. This is Thomas Traherne:

"Having been at the University and received there the taste and tincture of another education, I saw that there were things in this world of which I never dreamed; glorious secrets, and glorious persons past imagination. There I saw that Logic, Ethics, Physics, Metaphysics, Geometry, Astronomy, Poesy, Medicine, Grammar, Music, Rhetoric, all kinds of Arts, Trades and Mechanisms that adorned the world

78

pertained to felicity; at least there I saw those things, which afterwards I knew to pertain unto it; and was delighted in them. There I saw into the nature of the Sea, the Heavens, the Sun, the Moon and Stars, the Elements, Minerals, and Vegetables. All which appeared like the King's Daughter, all glorious within; and those things which my nurses, and parents, should have talked of there were taught unto me. Nevertheless some things were defective too. There was never a tutor that did professly touch Felicity, though that be the mistress of all other sciences. Nor did any of us study those things but as *aliena*, which we ought to have studied as our enjoyments."[1]

So it was for Traherne at Brasenose College, Oxford, in the sixteen-fifties: you had only to learn how to enjoy, and all literature (like every other study) was your proper material: for it was all, in its kind, revelation of God – "You never enjoy the world aright, till the sea itself floweth in your veins, till you are clothed with the heavens, and crowned with the stars: and perceive yourself to be the sole heir of the whole world, and more than so, because men are in it who are every one sole heirs as well as you. Till you can sing and rejoice and delight in God, as misers do in gold, and Kings in sceptres, you never enjoy the world."[2]

Most Christians would say that Traherne neglected the consequences of what is taught by the sixth belief relevant to literature and education, the Fall. He himself argued that the pains and difficulties of the fallen world make the world more to man than paradise was because "he is to learn a diviner art that will now be happy, and that is like a royal chemist to reign among poisons." In saying this, he makes his doctrine coincide closely with that at which his elder contemporary from Christ's College, Cambridge, John Milton, arrived by the exactly opposite route, laying great stress on the Fall. Milton says in *Areopagitica*:

"It was from out the rinde of one apple tasted, that the knowledge of good and evil as two twins cleaving together leapt forth into the World. And perhaps this is that doom which Adam fell into of knowing good and evill, that is to say of knowing good by evill. As therefore the state of man now is, what wisdom can there be to choose, what continence to forbear, without the knowledge of evill? He that can apprehend and consider vice with all her baits and seeming pleasures, and yet abstain, and yet distinguish, and yet prefer that which is truly better, he is the true warfaring Christian. I cannot praise a fugitive and cloistered virtue, unexercis'd and unbreath'd, that never sallies out and sees her adversary, but slinks out of the race, where that immortal garland is to be run for, not without dust and heat."

For such reasons, Milton argues against censorship of literature: there is implicit in his pamphlet a motive and a programme for an education by literature to moral ends. But most Christians would say that Milton neglects too much our, and the Lord's, prayer "Lead us not into temptation". Perhaps indeed both Traherne and Milton in their stress on what man can do, a little distort the seventh and last Christian belief relevant to literature and education, that of redemption, through Christ by grace.

Between these two extremes, of accepting all literature, indeed all experience, either as the revelation of God, or as the opportunity for man to exercise his freedom, there have, I think, been seven views among Christians as to what literature is a Christian's proper study, and as to how this comes about. They were for the most part originally formulated in the first centuries of Christian over against Greek and therefore pagan literature.

With such a contrast in mind, the first possible position is that in a fallen world the only redeemed and redeeming word of God is the Bible, and, given that the whole business of life is redemption, the Bible composes the only literature properly to be studied. This has been widely enough held, and indeed even more widely held has been the narrower variant that for most people only the Bible as it appears in liturgy and sermon is safe, necessary or desirable. Milton, moved perhaps by the passing away of the ideal Puritanical state to whose Parliament in its beginnings he had addressed *Areopagitica,* and by the restoration of a world, as he thought

> To good malignant, to bad men benign,
> Under her own weight groaning....[3]

makes his Christ, tempted by Satan with the wisdom, harmony and eloquence of Greek literature, reject it. Its philosophy is false: its poetry, stripped of its false "swelling epithets"

> Will far be found unworthy to compare
> With Sion's songs, to all true tastes excelling[4]

its oratory and political thought is far beneath that of the Hebrew prophets.

These exaltations of the Bible as literature are very tenable: but Milton only uses them as a second line to support an austere conviction new to him. For, says Christ in *Paradise Regained*

> He who receives
> Light from above, from the Fountain of Light
> No other doctrine needs, though granted true,[5]

and, even if only the Son of God has such light in its fullness, moreover,

> many books,
> Wise men have said, are wearisome, who reads
> Incessantly, and to his reading brings not
> A spirit and judgment equal or superior,
> (And what he brings, what needs he elsewhere seek?)
> Uncertain and unsettled still remains,
> Deep-versed in books and shallow in himself,
> Crude or intoxicate, collecting toys

And trifles for choice matters, worth a sponge;
As children gathering pebbles on the shore.[6]

Milton, in fact, is here attacking the idea of literary education altogether, and for good reasons, although for reasons which can only seem conclusive by exaggeration and question-begging. Only a very narrow concept of humanity and the world could suppose that the matter of the Bible contains everything that is desirable for a man to understand or know: only a very wild notion of inspiration could deny that light may descend from the fountain of light through other means than the Bible or one's inner conscience: and only a wilful naivety much unlike Milton's earlier subtle meditations (in *Areopagitica* and elsewhere) on temptation and experience, could argue that a man might bring to his reading, before ever he opened a book "a spirit or judgment equal or superior" to what might in trial, experience and thought mature in him as he reads.

Yet some such Puritan narrowness, and aversion to literature as literature, seems nearly indissociable from the restriction of education in literature to the Bible. It is a question not only of the obvious point of the small range, in relation to the whole body of possible knowledge, of the subject matter of the Bible: it is also a question of how the Bible has traditionally been supposed to be read, that is with primary attention to its presenting with authority a certain pattern of religious and ethical doctrine. This is not how we read literature as literature (though earlier thinkers such as Milton himself frequently talk as if they thought it was): and to think that it is how we should read literature or the Bible is to narrow one's ideas of reading, of inspiration, indeed of grace, and even of redemption.

To understand how else one might - how else one does in fact - read even the Bible, we must turn to other literature and to what further opinions have been held about the place of that in Christian education.

The second position that has been held from earliest times has granted that pagan literature is always suspect: but has argued from this that it is the duty of Christians to supplement the Bible by creating a literature which uses all the rhetoric and charm of fallen literature in the service of God. Caedmon, Sidney, Spenser and again Milton have done something of the sort in English. But it is notable that few or none of such attempts have been able to exclude in the end the pagan literature on which they drew.

One might, since the bulk of English literature is Christian literature, even if not always as consciously constructed over against pagan literature as by Caedmon or Milton, construct a university course in English literature with this principle in mind. Indeed, the course I followed at Oxford in the late nineteen fifties, from Aglo-Saxon to 1830, contained scarcely any non-Christian writers except some of the Romantics; and even they have a certain naturalness in them towards Christianity. C.S. Lewis, who helped to define that course, felt that the Romantics were a kind of ante-chamber to Christianity. But, although probably these considerations were present to Lewis's mind when he supported a syllabus with these limitations of time, I do not think they were conclusive even in his eyes, much less in those of the others who then supported or subsequently taught the course. And it is noteworthy that the feeling that non-religious writers - "Shaw and Wells and Mill and Gibbon and Voltaire" - were "a little thin; what as boys we called 'tinny'", lacking in "depth", and that "the roughness and density of life did not appear in their books" - this feeling was, or so Lewis claims in his autobiography, *Surprised by Joy*, arrived at empirically in his non-Christian days. Moreover his distinction is larger than the simple confinement to Christianity, including among the religious, "on whom I could really feed", Plato, Aeschylus, Virgil.[7] He belongs in fact to one of the classes I shall come to later, who have Christian criteria for preferring a certain kind of literature which may be doctrinally Christian or non-Christian.

It seems then that it is effectively impossible to hold the line of this second position. But here perhaps it is proper to note how much any course in English literature does teach of Christianity. The extreme case comes, not surprisingly, with medieval literature. I think I have not found any writer, not Dostoevsky, not even Shakespeare, who shakes and disturbs students as the author of *The Cloud of Unknowing* does. And someone who understood, alongside the four Gospels, *Piers Plowman*, the *Showings of Divine Love* of Lady Julian, and the *Cloud* itself would have nothing to learn of Christianity that can be learnt from books. But something similar is true of later periods, and even of what I suppose is the opposite, most godless extreme, the literature of the present day, English or European. In one of my recent tutorials, a girl remarked that "we" today do not think about God or evil or freewill, but that when we read books from the past like *Dr. Faustus* and *Paradise Lost* we are bound to. I recommended her to read Thomas Mann's *Doctor Faustus*. Even today, it is remarkable, and I think symptomatic of the state of England as I described it at the beginning, that our finest novelist, William Golding, and two of our three or four finest new poets, Geoffrey Hill and C.H. Sisson, while none certainly Christian, never cease to wrestle with Christian truths and feeling.

Mann's *Doctor Faustus* represents, though perhaps partly ironically, a school of thought argued today in such books as Rookmaaker's *Modern Art and the Death of a Culture,* which teaches that the urge or nisus of modernism is itself diabolic, disintegrative, turned towards nothing, darkness and evil. This is a Puritan opinion, overwhelmed by awareness of the Fall, and seems wholly to neglect the possibilities and power of God's grace in redemption. That power, I believe, it has never been given to man to express better in poetic form than to T.S. Eliot in the third and fourth sections of *Ash Wednesday,* a poem altogether modernist in style, language and mode of exploration of consciousness:

> Distraction, music of the flute, stops and steps of the
> mind
> > over the third stair,
> Fading, fading; strength beyond hope and despair
> Climbing the third stair.
> Lord, I am not worthy
> Lord, I am not worthy
> > but speak the word only.

That "strength beyond hope and despair" is grace; and the gap represented by the semicolon before it, between the irregular "stops and steps" and the assured movement of "Climbing ...", tries to enact the coming of grace, confirmed by the prayer at the end, the prayer for the response of God which is (as it happens) said before Communion. Eliot renders the prayer with another gap in it, and in some sense unfinished. In these gaps and silences the reader is left to experience, to accept or to deny what the words about them shape for him - the presence or the absence of God.

The irregularities, gaps and silences of this passage from *Ash Wednesday* represent something of the techniques of modernism. In this passage, it might be said, they offer to the believer an intimation of grace: to the unbeliever a choice - either an imagination of what the believer might mean by grace, or an attempt to imagine something secular and contained within the empirical psyche that might correspond to grace, or simply nothing. Eliot would not let poetry put its experiences forward as substitutes for religious experience.

But in other contexts, between other words, in Eliot's *The Hollow Men, Gerontion* or *The Waste Land,* these irregularities, gaps and silences intimate, clearly or less clearly, nothing, or chaos: more consistently so in the works of other modernists. And the kinds of experience which they then intimate - say in the works of Beckett - might be held undesirable on three possible grounds: first psychologically, in that they represent places in the mind which exist, and the imaginative exploration of which might in some circumstances drive readers into real madness, nihilism and despair. Secondly, in a literary sense, from an opposite angle, that they might cause readers to treat as a merely literary, and therefore relatively trivial experience, the abyss which may be nothing or God. As Lionel Trilling has put it, the abyss may seem to answer, with the gravity of all objects of serious study "Interesting, am I not?".[8] Thirdly and finally, theologically, in that a Godless sense of the world may be forced on the reader.

These are real possibilities, and raise real problems. The question of the bounds of proper study - how far can you go? - remains, however far these bounds are extended: in the case of literature however far you extend them beyond the Bible. But the problem here is not the same for a Christian as it would probably be for the adherent of any other faith. For all three of these possibilities exist for one of the nodal points of the Christian Bible: in the narrative in *Mark* and *Matthew* of the death of Christ and His cry "My God, my God, why hast thou forsaken me?" That cry might drive a Christian to despair, to atheism, or even to the bloodless discussions of scholarship.

Yet the opposite has been found, often enough, to be true: that this cry of despair has held for many people a sense that despair can be redeemed: that there is no pain in the world of His creation that God has not identified Himself with. Christ's cry, like Christ's death, can be the foundation of faith. Chesterton observed early in this century that the passion of Christ is the only symbol in any religion "in which God seemed for an instant to be an atheist":[9] and even in the great pagan works of modernism - in *The Waste Land* or *Waiting for Godot* - the passion remains, witnessing to its power to affect, perhaps to redeem, even atheism. The silences of modernism can be taken up into what Auden following Kierkegaard and Bonhoeffer speaks of:

> A silence on the cross
> As dead as we shall ever be
> Speaks of some total gain or loss
> And you and I are free
> To guess from the insulted face
> Just what Appearances He saves
> By suffering in a public place
> A death reserved for slaves.[10]

The limits of redemption, in literature as in life, cannot easily be defined.

The third possible approach to literary values would substitute for the theological criteria and boundaries of the second, ethical criteria and boundaries. This, which may appear to be a broadening, runs into the same questions: how far can you go? how far do you wish to go?

Literature, whether it proceeds from Christian or non-Christian, religious or non-religious sources, involves itself with ethical concerns and consequences, and may be classified as good or bad according to them. Literary study too may be regarded as training the student in ethical discernment. Milton in *Areopagitica* implies, as we have seen, just that, the mode of training being temptations entertained by the imagination. Other Christian writers have taken literature as conveying moral patterns in attractive form. "For even", says Sidney, " those hard-hearted evil men who think virtue a school name, and know no other good but *indulgere genio,* and therefore despise the austere admonitions of the philosopher, and feel not the inward reason they stand upon, yet will be content to be delighted – which is all the good fellow poet seemeth to promise - and so steal to see the form of goodness (which seen they cannot but love) ere themselves be aware, as if they took a medicine of cherries."[11] Matthew Arnold thought that poetry, as morality tinged with emotion, might even take the place of dogmatic religion: that the Bible itself was nothing else.

The difficulty with ethical formulations of what is good in literature is that they tend, either to leave the essence, the specific literariness of literature, in the realm of entertainment, as the cherries and not the medicine itself, or else to propound ethical canons which work in the realm of literature but seem inadequate to life. Speculation as to how imaginative experience relates to actual experience goes back at least to Plato: but there do not seem to be any very satisfactory ways of defining or predicting the relation. Leavis and his associates, Christian and non-Christian, come fairly close to the essence of literature, and propound theory of how good reading might lead to good moral choosing, in suggesting such canons as life, or sheer intelligence in dealing with moral matters, as criteria for good literature . Yet these canons do not seem to me capable of serving as primary ethical canons, as ultimate goods or ends. D.H.Lawrence, for example, undoubtedly offers a sense of life as a governing moral force: yet this seems as likely to destroy and corrupt an actual life - an actual marriage, say - as to exalt it. And fineness of moral discrimination is as likely when mediated through literature, as it is when simply taught, to degenerate into a bloodless but proud or angry Pharisaism.

Again, this kind of exaltation of sensitive literary response to a high moral status disintegrates in some hands into variants of the one ethical canon that everyone in this country and century recognises, freedom limited only by respect for my neighbour's freedom. I take it that the present pressures on literary studies from those immersed in structuralism, hermeneutics and post-structuralism, issue from the recognition that reading books need not promote freedom, but rather may deepen the hold of traditional canons of ethics on us, even when new expressions and new paradigms are provided for them. We have recognised, since the time of the romantics, what perhaps goes back to the sayings of Christ, that consciousness is better compared to a lamp than to a mirror, to a lamp giving out light which itself half forms what it sees. "Take heed therefore", the Light of the world said, "that the light that is in thee be not darkness."[12] It is this injunction that, according to their lights, our current reformers of literature, post-structuralist, feminist and neo-Marxist, attempt to fulfil. But I have not yet seen that their fundamental motivation is more than the urge to total freedom, and since this is only a negative canon, their efforts seem to issue in a destructive nihilism, or in a paradoxically constraining admiration only for literature politically concerned with liberation.

Nevertheless, what they are in search of, as I understand it, has much in common with what was finely analysed and upheld by R.G. Collingwood in his *Principles of Art:* and there is sound Christianity in his doctrine that true art purges the corrupted consciousness - the light that is darkness - of the society in which it arises. This doctrine comes, perhaps, as close as any variant of the view that the essential nisus of literature is moral can do, to doing justice to the essence of literature. It is striking that Collingwood found his paradigm of true art in Eliot's *The Waste Land.* For Eliot in *The Waste Land* and thereafter was concerned for the purgation and exploration simultaneously of both consciousness and language. It was, one might say, an awareness of the corrupted or fallen state of consciousness and language in his modernist and non-Christian time, the time of *The Waste Land,* which led him through his portrayal of the subtleties of consciousness and self-deception, through the irregularities and silences of which we have spoken, to the imagination of the action of grace in his

Christian and equally modernist life. Throughout his exploration he was assisted by an intuition of the connections between word as meaning language, word as meaning literature, and Word in the Johannine sense of Christ the creative power of God. In the poems of his non-Christian middle years he approaches as nearly as a great poet can do to the paradoxical achievement of presenting a language without an ordering meaning, a *logos,* in a world without ordering meaning - as in *Gerontion*

> The word within a word, unable to speak a word
> Swaddled with darkness.

This is the fallen aspect of our understanding, with which even the most orthodox Christian must come to terms, the aspect of the truth which Nietzsche and his followers among the post-structuralists have hold of. But it is doubtful whether a great poet, who must trust language, can reach absolute nihilism about language. Nietzsche well and double-edgedly remarked, "He who believes in grammar believes in God." Eliot found a path through the utmost possible nihilism that he could reach about meaning and language, to the Johannine and Platonic doctrine we have already touched on in Bede's prayer, which is expressed in *Ash Wednesday* and *Burnt Norton:*

> Words strain,
> Crack and sometimes break, under the burden....
> The Word in the desert
> Is most attacked by voices of temptation.....
> If the lost word is lost, if the spent word is spent
> If the unheard, unspoken
> Word is unspoken, unheard;
> Still is the unspoken word, the Word unheard,
> The Word without a word, the Word within
> The world and for the world;
> And the light shone in darkness and

> Against the Word the unstilled world still whirled
> About the centre of the silent Word.
> O my people, what have I done unto thee.

This last passage, from *Ash Wednesday,* builds up to, and relies like an arch on the last line, which is at once a phrase from the Bible and a phrase attributed in the liturgy to the crucified Christ. Both this passage, indeed, and the lines from *Burnt Norton* preceding it, rely, for their assertion of the possibility of a purged and trustworthy language, on the presence of revelation through God incarnate in the world. It would not be too much to say that while for Nietzsche to believe in grammar is to believe in God, for Eliot to believe in the possibility of expression or communication in language, at any level deeper than pointing or trading, is to believe in the incarnation of God.

Against all such ethical or theological exaltations of literature a reaction is possible which provides a fourth possible approach to literary values: to stress that literature is entertainment, at however high a level, and that neither the greatest of writers (Milton, Lawrence, Donne) nor the greatest of literature need suffer very much as sheer literature from advocating, imagining or enforcing quite wicked positions. In its pure form, which would reduce the study of literature either to the interesting but trivial history of a form of entertainment, or to the showing up of too pretentious ethical claims, this reaction need not detain us, being plainly false. Literature does, even if not predictably, have important ethical effects. This is implied, indeed, by the most plausible theory of its power as entertainment, that it enables us to exercise pleasant emotions, or discharge unpleasant or excessive emotions, in the realm of imagination, where one has, so to speak, to pay less for the exercise or the discharge. The difficulty with this theory is that it seems not to match our judgments as to what is greater or lesser literature: I certainly would count as the works of literature which allow me these operations most purely and which most predictably leave me in a state of supreme psychic well-being, the short stories of P.G. Wodehouse and of M.R. James. These are small masterpieces of art, and have, in my view more important ethical implications than they are usually given credit for: but neither I nor anyone have ever heard of, least of all their authors, would set them with *King Lear* or the book of *Job*. This sort of experience is, I think, common enough.

Nevertheless, the theory does provide a probable account of the way in which literature operates: and so can assist the ethical approach in its difficulties about the effect of imagination and reading on character and action, even if not very conclusively. And even apart from the difficult questions of the effect of literature on action, a Christian is bound to believe that what the heart and imagination entertain, for good or ill, has ethical importance: witness Christ's condemnation of the man who commits adultery in his heart. Equally important is the question of the man who entertains good imaginations at the expense of actions.

A fifth possible approach to literature, which does more justice than the ethical to the essence of literature, is already adumbrated in the passages from Eliot's poetry, and in the confused but rich passage from Sidney, as well as in the prayer of Bede. All three imply that it may be the function of literature to present the good, to present God, in a form not only to be understood more clearly, nor only to be rendered attractive by cunning adornment and literary technique - by cherries and delight - but in its most pure state - which seen, Sidney says, men cannot but love.

This position implies a Platonist, symbolising approach to literature which perhaps can best be adumbrated in Sir Thomas Browne's words:

"......even that vulgar and Tavern-Musick, which makes one man merry, another mad, strikes in me a deep fit of

Devotion, and a profound contemplation of the first Composer; there is something in it of Divinity more than the Ear discovers: it is an Hieroglyphical and shadowed Lesson of the whole world, and Creatures of God, such a melody to the Ear, as the whole world well understood, would afford the understanding. In brief, it is a sensible fit of that harmony, which intellectually sounds in the Ears of God."[13]

A bold saying, but not therefore to be despised: Lord David Cecil once applied it to the novels of Jane Austen, I think by way of making, as humbly as possible, the claim that the harmony of works that appear first as entertainment does claim part of the fallen or imperfect universe for the divine harmony, or recognise that harmony already existing, even where obscured.

This doctrine, though ultimately deduced from Plato, can be put in forms which do not in every way imply the Platonic doctrine of the absolutely existing idea of the good, nor the objective harmony Browne speaks of. It is certainly implicit in Coleridge's doctrine that consciousness with imagination, its secondary creative partner, is "a repetition in the finite mind of the eternal act of creation in the infinite I AM." [14] and in his correlative doctrine of the symbol as the means of revelation, a doctrine developed in relation to literature by Arthur Machen in his eccentric but most unfairly neglected book *Hieroglyphics*. Machen once again proposes a bound to literature: this time the distinction is with "journalism". Literature conveys ecstasy, embodied in symbolic form: journalism describes, recounts and analyses happenings from the world of everyday experience as it is normally assumed to be (which is not necessarily like what actually happens to anyone, as Machen is careful to say): from a more or less positivistically conceived world, one might say. It seems to me a recognisable distinction even in the polemic form Machen gives it, and even when

- conceding that journalism may be more intelligent, observant and psychologically perceptive, and written in a chaster style, than literature - he chooses for his example of journalism *Vanity Fair* and of literature *The Pickwick Papers.* The Christianity of the doctrine is made explicit by Machen when at the end of his book he points out that it is in a sense identical with Catholic, or rather sacramental theology. Its affinity is clear too with incarnational theology, in particular with the fifth of the doctrines we outlined at the beginning, the Athanasian article that the Word was made flesh, not by conversion of the Godhead into flesh, but by taking of the manhood into God. The symbol, the vehicle is raised to the expression of what in Machen's view is the thing symbolised, the tenor, ecstasy: ecstasy is not only a property of the things which arouse, or, better, convey it. Keats' *Ode to a Nightingale* is less like a machine to stimulate delight, than a sacrament.

If the symbolic school represents the Catholic, the sacramental stress within Christianity, the ethical school perhaps represents Protestantism. The views of Milton and Traherne, too, may be regarded as extreme endeavours in these two realms respectively, the attempt of Milton to extend the sphere of ethical education to all literature, of Traherne similarly to extend the sphere of education in sacramental or symbolic perception to all literature. Both symbolic and ethical, to my mind, embody real perceptions, real distinctions: but if both are partly valid, then it is clear that the absolute form of either, the total restriction of literature to either the ethical or the symbolic, cannot be. It is plain enough, too, that though some books and authors are more easily thought of in terms of one approach or the other, most are patient of either. I have for example lately read the remark, evidently intended as something to be taken for granted, that Dickens' novels "explore human behaviour in terms of social protest." It is a tenable view: clearly Machen would think of it as a

94

reduction of literature to journalism. Yet it must harmonise with the view that Dickens presents the sharp, bright, solid and gigantic world seen through the visionary eyes of childhood and expressed in imagery that is less that of protest than of humour.

What I think underlies both the ethical and the symbolic attempts to distinguish literature from something else has been expressed by C.S. Lewis in his *An Experiment in Criticism,* and provides my sixth approach. Lewis points out that most of us are familiar with a distinction, not primarily of kinds of books but of ways of reading. One kind of reading serves to pass the time, engages the attention on one level only, though for one reading it may engage attention very satisfyingly. In the other kind, we engage at many levels, we seem to touch, to draw refreshment from, immense depth. Perhaps the most telling example of the distinction happens when we suddenly remember, reading a book, that we have read it before - and return it to the library, give it away or at best scan very hastily to the end, picking out a few remembered phrases or passages. That book demands of us only to be read in the single-levelled way (except perhaps in the few remembered phrases); we shall never do so with a book that demands of us that it be read in the many-levelled way, or, as is most common with books of that kind, in both ways.

It is not a matter of obvious complexity: Lewis in *Surprised by Joy* cites the opening of a Hans Anderson story as affording endless enjoyment "How it did rain, to be sure",[15] and Machen gives as an example of "literature" almost the same simple remark from *The Pickwick Papers:*

> "How it snows," said one of the men, in a low tone.
> "Snows, does it?", said Wardle.
> "Rough, cold night, sir," replied the man; "and there's a wind got up, that drifts it across the fields, in a thick white cloud."[16]

Books demand of us to be read in one way or the other. This is no absolute distinction: as Lewis remarks, it may be that there is no book that has not been read by someone in the many-levelled way. If so, there are many more good books than we had thought - which, he says, "I reckon an advantage."[17] But it is an objective distinction nonetheless: many more people read Dickens in the many-levelled way than read Georgette Heyer, to name no very extreme contrast. Nor is the difference one of social habit or the fiat of an institution, but of what the books demand.

Although the distinction does, I think, provide an element common to both symbolic and ethical readings, the book which asks for reading at depth need be neither symbolic nor ethical, though it is likely to be one or the other or both. It might be flagrantly corrupting for some people in some circumstances - one might instance again the exaltation of the dark gods by D.H. Lawrence. A Christian who accepts Lewis's distinction may well hope that a literary education would wean readers from unthinkingly modelling their emotions on the situations in novels, and interpreting their feelings in the words of powerful writers: but weaning would only imply that one *need* not do these things, not that one would lose the capacity voluntarily to extend one's feelings by learning new words and new senses of words to express them.

For the real importance of this approach for Christian education is that it focuses attention on something even more of the essence of Christian ethics than the direction of passion or the attainment of integrity. The conspicuous mark of literature that engages our attention at depth is that it takes us out of ourselves. I do not say that this is invariable: I do think that it is normal. In poetry, the experience is at its most intense, being what Owen Barfield calls in his *Poetic Diction* "the felt change of consciousness."[18] In novels it may have that intensity, but is normally apparent in something more relaxed, one might say in slow motion, in the apprehension of what the world is through the eyes, not only of the novelist, but of his fictional characters.

And if poetry and novels train us in that kind of perception, then, as Lewis puts it, they heal the wound without destroying the privilege of individuality.[19] That in turn must mean that they can provide a training in a technique helpful to what cannot be taught at all, only given: the second commandment of Christ to "love your neighbour as yourself." In all forms of that commandment so far as I know, in Hebrew, in Greek, in Latin, in English, the "as" can mean "as much as", "in the same manner as" or "as if he were yourself." The last meaning will suggest that you should know what it is to see with his eyes, to know with his mind, to understand and speak with his language. "This abides," says Charles Williams, in his poem *Bors to Elayne, On the King's Coins,*

> that the everlasting house the soul discovers
> is always another's; we must lose our own ends;
> we must always live in the habitation of our lovers,
> my friend's shelter for me, mine for him....
> Dying each other's life, living each other's death.

The sixth approach to the teaching of literature, Lewis's approach, here merges into a seventh, that in which literature is a training in understanding and communication as the techniques of this life of what Williams called coinherence.

These techniques are important not only in understanding other people, but in understanding other cultures: something not only important in a country such as Britain now is, but part of the definition of being human. Man is the animal that has the unique capacity to understand symbol systems not his own: and literature is the embodiment of this capacity, and one of the principal means for

extending it. Chaucer, one of the first people of modern
times to understand the problem of understanding other
cultures, gives an apt summary in his *Troilus and Criseyde* of
the closeness of relation between understanding another
culture and understanding another person. You know, he
says, that

> in form of speech is change
> Within a thousand year, and wordes tho
> That hadden price, now wonder nice and strange
> Us thinketh hem, and yet they spake hem so,
> And sped as well in love as men now do.
> Eke for the winnen love in sundry ages,
> In sundry landes, sundry ben usages....
> Forthy men sayn, each country hath his lawes.
> Eke scarcely been there in this place three
> That han in love said like and done in all.[20]

It is a passage in which I am not sure what (in his time)
is the more startling, the realisation of the changes in
cultural fashion (in which some, such as Petrarch, had an-
ticipated him) or the implication that, nevertheless, they
may not be essentially different from the contrasts between
people in one milieu (which I think is entirely original).

Because the study of literature is a primary means to
understanding other human symbol-systems, and because
in such a study there is a strong affinity between
understanding other people and understanding other
cultures, this study of literature ought to include literature
from a culture as alien as is feasible for linguistic reasons or
for reasons of the coherence of a course. In connection
with English literature the most obvious are its ancestral literatures: medieval English, Anglo-Saxon, Latin, Greek and
Hebrew. In a Christian education Hebrew literature and
some Greek literature, in the original languages or in
translation, will have a special place: that is, the Bible.

It is at this point that it will be appropriate to fulfil the promise I made when discussing the first approach to literature, to say something of reading the Bible as a part of literature. And in most of what I have left to say, which concerns reading the literature of other cultures, and the idea of a literary canon, I shall take the Bible as my principal example, though most of my remarks will refer to all literature.

It is a question of which we are now very conscious, how far its arising in the forms of an ancient and partly alien culture affects our reading of the Bible. Some would say it does so to a nearly crippling degree. I believe this to be nonsense: if the degree of misunderstanding were crippling we should not be making sense of the Bible at all, let alone finding ourselves moved by it.

It is of course true that even from the most purely aesthetic point of view, let alone the ethical and the religious, we disregard the meanings of alien words and ways at our peril. A colour blind man, however sensitive he may be to drawing and line, cannot assess the mass and balance of a painting. He is blind not only to its colour but to its form. He may contrive to see it as partly perfect, and the whole of it as having a kind of consistency, but a perverse and unsatisfying one. If he received the gift of seeing colours, what he would see would no longer be marked by oddness but by a shock of strangeness and life.

But the analogy is in the end hopeful. For it is with a shock of strangeness and life that we do in fact receive Chaucer's *Troilus and Criseyde,* Sophocles' *Trachiniae,* Virgil's *Aeneid,* and above all *Job,* the Psalms, the Gospels, *Isaiah.* W.H. Auden once observed that you should never ask "Have you read any good books lately?" but "Have you been read by any good books lately?" There is plainly an affinity with Lewis's second mode of reading, reading in depth, in this idea: but Auden was extending to literature in general an aphorism which he printed in his *Faber Book of Aphorisms:*

"We do not criticise the New Testament: it criticises us."

Books in general, the Bible in particular, break in on us, judge us, break and reform our responses. And with structures as complex as those which I have mentioned, *Troilus and Criseyde, The Trachiniae,* the *Aeneid, Job* and the rest, in which not only does every word spark off a new set or responses, but every combination of words, and every combination of a combination, it is not credible that our continued delight and compelled awe are based on substantial misunderstandings. Overall the irruption of which I have spoken makes a way for truth, whatever particular misreadings and misunderstandings may occur, however much in reading Job or the *Aeneid* we may recognise the need for the services of criticism and scholarship. Our naive responses remain the primary datum: the fact that we have a naive response at all is an overwhelmingly important testimony to our perceiving, not a chaos whose interconnections are lost, but the original and real structure. For a poem or a romance is a closely interlocking pattern of words and meanings, and the interlockingness of the contexts is both a strong testimony to the validity of the responses which the pattern elicits, and a means to the preservation of both single and complex meanings. When a reader takes up the meaning of a word or a phrase in a poem and inhabits it, in that moment and thereafter some areas of meaning, which in ordinary contexts he would presume, are denied to him by its present context; in that moment and thereafter he is gestured towards rooms in experience that he did not know even existed; as he proceeds even through one sentence, much more a whole passage, he may find previously unknown, still hardly knowable, demands laid upon him. Often enough the naive responses are mistaken, but any hypothesis, such as it is the business of scholarship to formulate, that suggests this, has the burden of proof laid on it.

Let me give a perhaps too simple example of what would

take half a lifetime to justify properly. The Lord in His prayer asks τὸν ἄρτον ἡμῶν τὸν ἐπιούσιον δὸς ἡμῖν σήμερον. From the time that the dialect of Hellenistic Greek which the Gospels use fell out of use, until the study of the papyri of Oxyrhynchus eighty years ago, all scholarship would confirm that this means "Give us today our supersubstantial bread" as the official Latin renders it. Something about the simplicity of its context kept alive the improbable tradition that the phrase meant, as scholarship now agrees, "Give us today our daily bread."

I would in this discussion assimilate the mode of reading the Bible to the mode of reading any great literature, not because I do not think the Bible unique - I do - but because I think that its uniqueness is not extrinsically, or arbitrarily, or socially established, but intrinsic, and recognisable in the act of reading it as we read other books.

This is a controversial position. Lewis's distinction of modes of reading is paralleled by Abba Matta El Meskeen of the Monastery of St. Macarius in Egypt in an article, "How to read the Bible":

"There are two ways of reading:
The first is when a man reads and puts himself and his mind in control of the text, trying to subject its meaning to his own understanding and then comparing it with the understanding of others.
The second is when a man reads putting the text on a level above himself trying to bring his mind into submission to its meaning, and even setting up the text as a judge over him, counting it as the highest criterion.
The first way is suitable for any book in the world, whether it be a work of science or of literature. The second is indispensable in reading the Bible. The first way gives man mastery over the world, which is his natural role.
The second gives God mastery as the all-wise and all powerful Creator. But if man confuses the roles of those

101

two methods, he stands to lose from them both, for if he reads science and literature as he should the Gospel he grows small in stature, his academic ability diminishes and his dignity among the rest of creation dwindles.

And if he reads the Bible as he should read science, he understands and feels God to be small, the divine being appears limited and His awesomeness fades. Man acquires a false sense of his own superiority over divine things and this is the very same forbidden thing that Adam committed in the beginning."[21]

But, unlike Lewis, Abba Matta El Meskeen would prescribe his modes of reading extrinsically, before the books are open. This I think is a mistake. It is better that a book and its reader decide between each other into which category their relation falls: prescription falsifies the act of reading and produces counterreactions such as constantly pervert Biblical scholarship. A false reverence, and a false scepticism countering it, have between them so affected us that it requires effort to read the Bible cleanly. It is now the urgent task of Christian critics to find ways in which this can be done: to destroy obstacles to the kind of reading of which Coleridge said "that in the Bible there is more that finds me than I have experienced in all other books put together; that the words of the Bible find me at greater depths of my being......"[22]

What is true eminently of the Bible is true of all literature that has in any sense been given canonical status: the identical phenomena are known with Shakespeare. I saw this year a list of personal statements about modes of studying his works which ranged from "to *try* to efface ourselves before a work of art and feel addressed by it, rather than simply addressing it" at one extreme, as far as "to interrogate rather than to appreciate or celebrate his work, i.e..... to examine critically the reasons for his status."

Here again, though for myself I would say the former is

the way in which Shakespeare most commonly requires to be read, it seems a pity to state it beforehand, and likely to generate the other response by reaction. Yet they could so generate each other as to work in harmony. In actual teaching, perhaps they do.

For what in a tutorial or a seminar way of teaching does one do? The teacher suggests an angle, preferably stimulating, and a reading list. The student reads and presents what arises from the reading in an essay. The teacher asks questions to clarify first, and then asks the other students present for their questions and comments. As the discussion proceeds, the teacher enlarges upon the points of the original essay, to see if they could be put better, and developed, to find, if necessary, what whole organic theory was implicit in the essay: finally offers what case can be put against the essay - whether according to the teacher's own views or not - and how the student can deal with the attack. Finally, with luck, the teacher can sum up in a way which generates the angle to be considered at the next meeting, or, with even more luck, a student will do so.

Such is a literary education, is it not? Or is ideally. In this sort of discussion the multifarious difficulties we have touched on in this lecture should find their fulfilment and resolution. In such a discussion "He who is not against me is for me" is found implicit and even "Love your neighbour as yourself." Of course the ideal is not found much more in a literary education than anywhere else on earth. Yet Langland said in *Piers Plowman* that if heaven on earth is to be found anywhere, it is in a school. In terms of learning to understand and to communicate, if a literary education is working at all, it ought to be proving that highly religious statement true.

Some parts of this lecture are dependent on my *The Later Middle Ages* (Methuen, 1981), *An Anatomy of Consciousness: a Study of the poetry of T.S. Eliot as a single poem* and *To All True Tastes Excelling: an Essay on reading the Bible as a book* (Harvester Press).

Notes

1. Thomas Traherne, *Centuries of Meditations, III*, 36 & 37.
2. op. cit. *I*, 29.
3. *Paradise Lost, XII* 538-9.
4. *Paradise Regained, IV*, 343 & 346-7.
5. op. cit. *IV*, 289-90.
6. op. cit. *IV*, 321-30.
7. *Surprised by Joy*, ch. xiv.
8. Trilling, L., *Beyond Culture*, "On the Teaching of Modern Literature."
9. *Orthodoxy*, ch. viii.
10. "Friday's Child".
11. Sidney, *Apology for Poetry*.
12. *Luke, XI*, 35.
13. *Religio Medici, II*, 9.
14. *Biographia Literaria, I*, xiii.
15. *Surprised by Joy*, ch. x.
16. *The Pickwick Papers*, ch. xxvii.
17. *An Experiment in Criticism*, ch. xi.
18. *Poetic Diction*, ch. ii et seq.
19. *An Experiment in Criticism, Epilogue.*
20. *Troilus and Criseyde, II*, 22-8, 42-4.
21. *Fairacres Chronicle*, 15, 3, pp. 17 f; from *St Mark*, November 1981, pp. 1f.
22. *Confessions of an Enquiring Spirit*, Letter 2.

Education, Religion and Social Science:
An Islamic Approach

Ilyas Ba-Yunus

Social sciences as they are taught in the universities and colleges these days, represent the latest contribution that Western civilization has made to human intellect. Including sociology, psychology, social and cultural anthropology, social and human geography, economics, political science and history, they differ from earlier social and political philosophy in that they insist on generating and analyzing data through the application of scientific method in reaching generalized conclusions.

My purpose in this paper is to present what one may call an Islamic approach to social sciences rudiments of which are already found in the works of classical Islamic writers. More recently, it is reasserting itself in the writings of several Muslim social scientists, most of whom are trained in the West (for instance, see Al-Faruqi, 1981; Ba-Yunus, 1977, 1981; A.H. Siddiqui, 1981; M.N. Siddiqui, 1981a, 1981b; K. Siddiqui, 1981 and many others).

As Marsh (1976:19) pointed out, contemporary sociology "has been developed in a small corner of the world and may, therefore, be highly limited as a universal scheme". What is true of sociology, is also true of social science in general. Or, to redescribe Al-Faruqi (1981:16), the Western social scientist claims "to be objective when he in fact is prejudiced, to be complete when he is in fact reductionist, to talk about human society when he is in fact referring to Western society, of religion when he is in fact referring to Christianity, or of social and economic laws when he is in fact referring to common practices of some Western societies". However, a central concern of Muslim students of modern social sciences is that these sciences have not merely ignored Islam, indeed, they have an in-built bias against it. Edward Said's *Orientalism* (1978) brings out this very point quite succinctly. Others have made similar observations (for instance, Turner on Max Weber, 1974). Whatever the nature of bias against Islam in contemporary social sciences, I think that a great deal of this bias can be explained in terms of the development and the nature of these sciences, especially with respect to religion in general.

Social Science and Religion

Social sciences have at least one thing in common with religion in general. It is their preoccupation with the solutions of the problems of men living together in entities called society. Each religion in its own way, and each social science area in its own way, have something significant to say about these problems. It is unfortunate that instead of being supportive, they fall apart. In the West, this rivalry between the two is not in terms of rivalry between two equal. In this age of science religion, specially that in the West, has been reduced to a position of being a reluctant follower of what goes on in society. The same relationship is discernible between social sciences and religion. For instance, while it is not uncommon for the churches to invite social scientists to address church gatherings, we hardly see priest or clergy being invited to give lectures in social science classes. Whereas, many a clergy or prospective clergies are these days taking courses in social sciences, we hardly see Social Science students, even those who are going to specialize in religion, attending religious seminaries. While it is not uncommon for the clergies to refer to the works of social scientists in their writings and even in their sermons, it is rare for a social scientists to refer to the works of religious ministers and the priests. In fact, there is no religiously based tradition or school of thought in geography, economics, psychology, and political science, as there is none that I know of in history. Those who cared to pay attention to religion in their studies (sociologists and cultural anthropologists in particular), remained bogged down with the behavioural questions of individual religiosity or the functional relationship between religion and other institutions of society. The assumption underlying such studies is that religion is just one of the many things, mostly at the receiving end of the spectrum, that people do in society. It has seldom occurred to the social scientists that religious doctrines may provide assumptions that may be sociologically, economically, politically and even psychologically most meaningful; and that a social science analysis of such doctrines might not only give new outlooks to the social science, it may also increase and enhance social science understanding of the religious doctrines regarding human nature and the nature of human family, society and history. On the other hand, Karl Marx,   an ideologue, an activist and the principal originator of the international socialist movement - has been analyzed and reinterpreted as to his sociological, political, economic and historical doctrines so much so that some of his assumptions regarding polity, economy and history have become the basis of the so-called conflict theory in sociology and political science. Our understanding of socialist ideology is enhanced not merely because there have been some revolutionary activities under the banner of socialism, but mainly because socialism became an important school of thought in a number of social science disciplines.

However, there does not exist a comparable approach, say, a Christian theory in sociology or a Calvinistic theory of work and this despite Max Weber. No wonder sociology of religion is one of the least developed areas within the general field of sociology.

Does it mean that religious doctrines do not have anything significant to contribute to our understanding of societal behaviour? Or, is it that the contemporary social scientist has an inbuilt bias against any claim which is primarily God centered? The fault seems to lie with the social scientists who have developed a tradition of distancing themselves from religion in their analysis of human behaviour. There are two closely related but quite distinct sources of this social science ambivalence towards religion. One of them is the circumstances in which social sciences were conceived, and the other is the social science enchantment with scientific methodology.

The Origin of Western Social Science

The social science non-religiosity, if not irreligiosity, is a direct result of the desire on the part of social scientists to mimmick and unquestioningly follow the methodology of the physical and natural sciences. Success in physical sciences brought about a great deal of prestige and other rewards to its practitioners in the late 18th and the 19th century Europe, at the same time that industrialization was demanding more scientific discoveries and breakthroughs. Coupled with this, there pervaded among physical scientists a feeling of being able to have acquired the method of mastery over nature and a sense of pride which could evoke a sort of 'sibling rivalry ' among colleagues in the neighbouring disciplines. Specially those in the fields of sociopolitical philosophies could not remain unmoved by this dazzling progress of science much longer. Thus, mastery over nature and the material benefits, we are told, did not solve the problems of society. Conscious efforts were made to prove that they grew worse, not so much in spite of, but exactly because of, material progress under science and technology. The lost pride could be regained by proving that scientific method could be extended to social analysis as well in order to solve the growing problem of living together. The honour could be restored by assuming the role of the pundits who could first scare the daylight out of a materially prospering society and, then, following it on with the "rabbit out of hat" solutions.

It was in this atmosphere of envy and hope that August Comte introduced his "positive philosophy " in which he delineated the new approach for the study of social relationship among people. The dismembered religion-based moral philosophy of the past had to be buried for good. From then on truth had to be discovered not in the religious dogma but in the scientific empiricism. A new prophet was born with scientific tools he did not quite know how to handle.

Social Science and Scientific Method

One could still tolerate social science attitude toward religion had these sciences been successful in employing the methodology that they borrowed from physical and natural sciences. In that case these sciences perhaps could not unsettle religious beliefs in the West more than the damage rendered the Christian cosmological doctrines by the physical and natural sciences. However, continued reliance on physical science methodology on the part of social sciences has proved to be a heavy baggage rather than an asset over time. If this has been true in the analysis of major areas of social life, it is even more true in the analysis of religion.

The subject matter of science varies from one area to another. Likewise, scientists adopt, devise and innovate various techniques which facilitate their specific enquiries. However, there are at least two psychological strands which characterize all scientific methods irrespective of the area of interest or specific research projects. Both have been consciously but erroneously adopted by the social scientists. One of them is scepticism and the other objective neutrality.

First, science is public and open to questioning. This means that there is nothing sacred in science and that every proposition has the liability of being rejected. Observations which form the basis of any propositions are to be replicated, meaning thereby that truth has only limited span of life. As data collecting techniques improve over time, refined data do not necessarily conform to the older ones. This is how science staged a devastating attack on Christian cosmological beliefs and this is how older scientific theories are rejected, modified and new propositions generated. The scepticism of physical science remained almost a latent tendency among physical and natural scientists until it was "discovered" and vocalized by the students of positive philosophy. No social science discourse on methodology of research is without at least a mention of scepticism as a matter of scientific virtue.

Secondly, objects of study in physical and natural sciences are "dead" in the sense that they do not react to the scientist's probe and that they do not evoke any sense of like or dislike, sympathy or antipathy or any other kind of emotional involvement of the observer or the scientist himself. Even when the scientist is dealing with live matters like animals, say, mice, he may subject them to painful and often fatal experiments without himself going through any emotional convulsions. Of course, objects like plants or rocks do not at all arouse any such feelings in him. Thus a physical or a natural scientist is able to keep his psychological distance from his objects of study. He does not feel any affinity with them. Neither do they provoke any animosity in him. This leads him to record behaviour of his objects without any contamination from his own personal beliefs or biases. ˙

On the other hand, the main objects of study in social sciences are human beings and what they do in interaction with other humans. Most often social science data are collected by means of rather close encounter with the subjects. There are two difficulties with such studies. First is the subject bias and the other is the observer bias. In the first case whether one is speaking of social psychological experiments or sociological, demographic, economic or public opinion surveys, it is generally recognized that subjects react to the presence of the observer or the social scientist himself. These reactions are difficult to predict and often impossible to control. Consequently, social science texts have not gone beyond merely warning and sensitizing the researcher about these difficulties; but little has been or is being done about removing these difficulties from social science research. Most researchers simply forget about it in practice and most social science readers do not make any fuss about it either. I have yet to convince myself that the subjects of my doctoral research did not cheat me in their responses about their shoplifting behaviour. However, none of those eminent scholars in my doctoral committee raised even one question about this possibility in criminological surveys. It is like a folk disease which becomes so widespread that people stop defining it as a disease. However, this misperception does not solve the issue. It only makes social sciences findings suspect in the eyes of its critics.

However, observer bias in social science studies poses even more serious a problem. Making value judgements about others' activities, their beliefs, even their looks, is universally a fundamental part of human socialization. Social scientists, very much like other human beings, make value judgements about people whom they experience through interaction, whether directly or indirectly. Thus, Whites studying Blacks or Blacks studying Whites, Westerners studying the Orient or the Oriental studying the West and those from the Middle Class studying the Lower Class - all provide us with studies which are biased to varying degrees. Much the same arguments may be extended to the

111

media coverage of the "newsworthy" events. Whereas, those in the Third World in general, and the Islamic World in particular, have been increasingly critical of the Western media coverage of their societies, Moltoch and Lester (1975) found that even in news selection, media establishment is often biased in favour of powerful people and groups. While we are informed about various strategies which are and can be used to minimize the respondent or the subject bias, we are only left guessing about the bias of the observer himself. How much confidence can we entertain in studies in which the main source of bias is the observer himself?

Subject or respondent bias in social science research is serious enough; but the consequence of the observer bias is far reaching. While an unbiased physical scientist can afford to be sceptical as well as remain objective in his observation, the social scientist cannot afford to be both at the same time. In physical sciences, scepticism has come to mean the practice of scrutinizing and criticizing which is aimed at further refinement of existing propositions. In social sciences, more often it comes to assume its dictionary meanings. In physical sciences, scepticism generates a null hypothesis which is to be rejected or accepted as the data dictate. On the other hand, scepticism on the part of social scientist is often a result of and, I strongly suspect, has, a multiplier effect upon his pre-existing biases which then come to dictate where and how the data may be selectively collected and interpreted. Is it then very curious that social sciences research often ends up proving what the researcher wanted to prove to begin with? What is curious is that despite this problem, social science Gurus with few peripheral protests from time to time, continue to cling to their existing research strategies and vague propositions; and this despite their failure in providing any viable solution to the problems of societal living, whether they be economic, political or interpersonal and psychological.

Islam and Social Science

The above discussion should explain why Muslim students of social science are becoming wary of modern social sciences. Evidently, scepticism and faith do not mix. The scientist who looks with scepticism at religious claims only ends up developing research strategies which serve his pre-existing anti-religious social sciences biases. Further, because Western social scientists in general are used to casting all other religions in the image of Western Christianity, their anti-religious biases are extended to other religions as well, including Islam. Hence the need for a social science which would help Muslims understand their religion, their increasingly complex society and how their religion could come to grips with their contemporary problems.

Muslim Social Scientists and the 'Ulamā'

From the beginning, the Muslim *ummah*, or the world community of Islam, has always had and still has numerous *'ulamā'* or "men of knowledge" who have been looked up to for guidance throughout its turbulent history. They are the ones whose main preoccupation has been the discovery and rediscovery of the prescriptive body of configurations (which and which alone are to be defined as Islam in the strict sense of the word) by going back to the *Qur'ān* and the history of the Prophet and his companions and by reinterpreting them in the light of the then existing conditions of the Muslim *ummah* and the environment around it. As is evident, although they were jurists as far as the end product of their efforts is concerned, yet they could not be good jurists unless they also were adept in historical and social analysis. Those, Muslims as well as non-Muslims, who are proud of rediscovering Ibn Khaldun in modern times, seem to have chosen not to see that his views on and his methodology of history and civilization were actually the culmination and systematization of only a part of the long tradition of the juristic discourse among Muslim *'ulamā'*. Thus, the role of the *'ulamā'* in what constitutes Islam today, can not be minimized.

However, as Al-Faruqi (1981:6) put it:

> Modern times have increased tremendously the complexity of human life, necessitating a great amount of preparation for successful governance of life. As guides and leaders endowed with clear perception of the Muhammadan vision, of the wisdom the fathers displayed in their figurizations, and of the knowledge of modern realities, the Muslim social scientists are the *'Ulamā'* of the *Ummah* today. They are the planners of its strategies and designers of its future, the educators of the *Ummah* at large as well as of its political, social and economic leadership.

Even if some might dispute with Al-Faruqi for presenting a rather ambitious scheme regarding the role of Muslim social scientists in contemporary Islam, it does highlight the indispensability of the role of social science in the juristic activity on which the whole structure of Islam rests in the modern and a highly complex world today.

Cast in this role, the main purpose of the Muslim social scientist is not so much to refine and redefine the scope of social sciences as we know them today. Their main purpose, as Al-Faruqi put it, is "the study of the *ummah* in all its activities as an *ummah*" (1981:7). Writing about Islamic sociology, Ba-Yunus and Ahmad (1983) present almost the same argument. According to them, Islamic sociology has three main areas to be developed in future. First is theoretical i.e., a search through Islamic literature including the *Qur'an* and *Ḥadīth* (sayings of the Prophet) for deriving the basic assumptions of Islamic sociology. Second is critical

114

i.e., a research strategy based on comparative methodology aimed primarily at measuring the direction and the degree of deviance of Muslim (even non-Muslim) society from the Islamic ideals. Third is strategic i.e., a programme of action as to how this deviance could be minimized. I shall discuss this plan again in the following pages.

Where and How to Start?

It should be understood by now that here we are not dealing with a secular science. Very much like the Marxist approach in social sciences, Islamic social science starts with a value commitment. For instance, Syed Ali Ashraf, writes:

> If the Qur'ānic concept of the relationship be-
> tween morality and historical events and the
> Qur'ānic narration of the past are ignored, a
> Muslim historian can not attempt to formulate
> an Islamic concept of history. Similarly, an Is-
> lamic school of sociology cannot emerge if Mus-
> lim sociologists do not analyse their data with ref-
> erence to the Qur'ānic concept of absolute val-
> ues and human rights, duties and obligations. In
> the same way, it is impossible to create an Islamic
> school of psychology if the Qur'ānic concept of
> human nature, including the idea of the relation-
> ship between body, self and spirit, and man's
> destiny as the vicegerent of God on Earth, is
> overlooked, evaded or ignored. The same is true
> for economics and political science because
> neither the capitalist, interest-controlled eco-
> nomic system, nor the rigid regimentation of the
> Marxist economy and political system, can be
> acceptable to a Muslim. (1981:3)

Does it mean that only Muslims can contribute to Islamic social science? Are non-Muslims barred from entering the domain? On the surface at least, this seems to be the case. This is so because nearly all those who wrote on this subject had only a Muslim audience in mind. However, this does not necessarily have to be the case. In fact, there is little by way of asserting that the "insider" perspective is preferred to an "outsider" one, to use Merton's (1973) distinction. Should only Muslims be qualified to practise this discipline, then, as Vander Zanden (1979:441) put it "we could also argue that only monogamists should study monogamy; only confirmed democrats, democracy, and only dedicated capitalists, capitalism". To put it the other way, just as one does not have to be a socialist to be a Marxist or conflict sociologist, so one does not have to be a Muslim to be a contributor to Islamic social science. Edward Said (1978) and Bryan Turner (1974) are not Muslims and yet their writings have a great deal of inspiration for Muslim social scientists. Moreover, Islam is an open religion. It is by its very claim *"Hudan Lil Nās"* i.e. guidance for mankind. Islamic social science, therefore, cannot be restricted to Muslims only. There is many a Muslim social scientist who still may not believe in anything like Islamic social science. On the other hand, any non-Muslim who has come to understand the spirit and the logic behind Islamic doctrines, may make significant contributions in this direction. To begin with, I would say that of the three areas delineated by Ba-Yunus and Ahmad (1973), non-Muslim social scientists can make significant contributions towards critical research comparing actual Muslim practices with the Islamic commandments. Already, some non-Muslim social scientists have made significant contributions along the lines that I am proposing (among others, see Hoeble, 1961; Korson, 1968; and Esposito, 1982).

Principles of Islamic Social Science

Like any other scientific discipline, I envisage Islamic social

116

science discipline divided into three main areas: theoretical, research and applied. However, whatever the discipline, these social sciences gravitate around a generally agreed upon assumption among Muslim intellectuals, namely that Islam is an ideology and not merely a ritualistic worshipping formula. It is a total way of life (Qur'ān calls it *Dīn*) which covers all crucial aspects of social life including economic, political, interpersonal and even personal and spiritual.

At the theoretical level, this ideology has to be explained and reinterpreted as to its meaning. In research, actual behaviour of Muslims (even non-Muslims) has to be compared with the ideological prescriptions. In applied aspects, juristic reforms, evolutionary plans and even revolutionary changes fall in the area of Islamic social science.

Theoretical

As an ideology, Islam is the culmination of a long chain of the Divine message given to mankind through a succession of prophets. Long before Hegel, *Qur'ān* provided a dialectical view of human history. This view presents the evolution of mankind through a series of conflicts between those who were the bearers of the Divine message and those who always opposed these prophets. As a prophet was able to establish a just order, his disciples and descendants would soon forget and contaminate the true message. Hence the need for another prophet who would establish a new order under the Divine guidance congruent with the cultural evolution of human society. Finally, at certain junctures in human history came the last and the most comprehensive formula of societal life - Islam - through Prophet Muhammad.

This ideology is based on a number of doctrines the most important of which says, "There is no god but only one God, and Muhammad is His Prophet". This doctrine

117

occupies the central place in Islam. Without believing in and professing this doctrine, one cannot be a Muslim. This means that for one to be a Muslim merely the acceptance of the unity of God is not enough. Acceptance of the Prophethood of Muhammad is as important.

In fact, acceptance of the Prophethood of Muhammad means automatically that one would also believe in the existence of one God. Thus to prove the existence of God, a Muslim does not necessarily have to argue about the clock and the clock maker. The unity of God is to be proved through the Prophethood of Muhammad.

How do you know that Muhammad was a Prophet? How was it that his contemporaries recognized him as a Prophet? In the Muslim world, a Prophet is defined as a person who is a messenger of God. In his personal character a prophet is an embodiment of steadfastness and self sacrifice. More than that, prophets have generally been recognized by the miracles that God bestowed upon them.

For Muslims all over the world, Muhammad was a Prophet of God not only because of his personal character but also because of his very unusual miracle - the *Qur'ān* itself. Muhammad was an illiterate person. Before his Prophethood, he was known as *Al-Amīn*, as honest person, but never as a philosopher, always a man of action and not at all a literary person. With Prophethood, he astonished people with the literary power of the revelation and its philosophy. For people who knew him as an unlettered man, the Qur'ānic revelation came as a big surprise. Although Muhammad also spoke as an ordinary human being, as a teacher and as a planner, but those who speak Arabic as their mother tongue even today, are able to distinguish between his utterances as a man and the *Qur'ān* which also came out of his mouth.

In short, for his contemporaries, Muhammad was a miraclous man because an unlettered person could not even be expected to preach a new and a complete system with a highly informed historical analysis and with a literary power to support it. Once the Prophethood of Muhammad is recognized, then his teachings are accepted as doctrines. Of course, the most basic lesson he gave was "There is no god but only one God".

It is mainly in terms of this doctrine alone that the practice of Islam, individually and collectively can be explained. Thus, the question as to why Muslims marry the way they do, or why they believe in prophethood of Jesus, can be answered by referring to God through His message - the *Qur'an* - and the Prophet, through his practice of this message.

However, the *Qur'an* and the *Sunnah* (actions of the Prophet) do not constitute social science. The basic assumptions of Islamic social sciences have to be, therefore, derived from the word of God and the words and deeds of the Prophet. It is these assumptions that we now turn to.

Assumption 1. *The Nature of Nature:* Because God is the creator and the sustainer of the whole universe, everything in the universe operates according to His law. Thus, we reject all those statements which replace God's law with what they call nature, for instance "according to the dictates of nature....", "nature takes its course......." or "nature makes it possible.......". If we have to use the term nature at all, it should be understood that nature of anything is nothing but the Divine law according to which it operates. To put it differently, nature itself is the creation of God.

Assumption 2: *The Nature of Man:* Human nature may be described in terms of three characteristics which may be derived directly from the *Qur'an*.

First, man is made up of the opposites. In his make-up, God breathed into his body "made of sounding clay" "from His Own Spirit". These two elements in his make-up are supposed to represent urge toward evil and predisposition

119

toward good respectively (Shariati, 1979:4). This assumption is contrary to the Christian belief which views man as
being essentially a sinner.

Secondly, the above features of human make-up presume the existence in man of free will and the ability to
make his own decision. It means that his predispositions are
not pre-determining. What determines human action in
either of the two directions is the actor's will itself. This
assumption rejects all kinds of deterministic views whether
they be economic, social, psychological or biological. In the
broad terms, what it means is that human existence describes a process of continuously being caught between the
horns of never ending dilemmas and trying to escape from
them - in conforming or deviant directions. This very
process of choosing also implies the power of abstract
reasoning i.e. , as a matter of self conversing, man is able to
tell himself as to the relationship of different elements in
his environments and as to how they could be used or
escaped from.

Thirdly, man has been given the ability to learn and
acquire knowledge. The verse, 'And Allah taught Adam
"the names" '(Qur'ān, 2:31), is interpreted by most *'ulamā'*
as pointing to this very ability in man. There seems to be
general agreement that "the names" in this verse refer to
knowledge. Further, it may be said that this ability is not
only to acquire knowledge but also to produce knowledge
and increase his existing intellectual capacity. In this regard, it may not be out of place to mention that Qur'ān
urges man to explore the universe not in order to create
destruction (which he might do any way) but mainly in
order to explore the purpose behind God's creation. For
instance:

> Verily in the creation of the heaven and the
> Earth; and in the alternation of day and night,
> there are signs for the more thoughtful who

remember God while standing, sitting and prostrating and think about the creation of the heavens and the Earth and say, "Our Lord, you did not create this in vain...."

(3:191)

Search for knowledge has also been emphasized by the Prophet himself. For instance, he urged his followers to go "even up to China" in pursuit of knowledge.

Assumption 3: The Nature of Society: According to the *Qur'an*, human society started with one man and one woman (Adam and Hawwā). This assertion rejects any claims that man appeared at several places on this Earth. From this humble beginning, the *Qur'an* traces the evolution of human society through *qabāil* (tribes), *shu'ub* (communities) and finally *ummah* (nations).

Whatever its demographic and cultural development over time, *Qur'an* focuses on four major structural features which quite plausibly appear to provide the least common denominators of human society universally. Called institutions in modern social science language, these features are the family, polity, economy, and worship. Although it also deals with a number of extra institutional aspects of social action, the *Qur'an* reserves special and often detailed treatment for these constellations of collective activities. Thus forcing a sociological conclusion upon us, namely, that *no collectivity may be defined as society unless it operates on the basis of these four institutions to say the least*. As far as I know, this definition of society as derived from the *Qur'an* has not been extended by any other sociologist so far.

Now as we know, social institutions represent collective expectations. Hence, they also possess a collective weight thus dictating if not completely determining individual character of people in society.

Assumption 4. *Nature of Human Action:* As a corollary to the above assumption, we may now see that despite his wilfulness, in his action man is neither fully free nor is he fully constrained. On the other hand, society is neither completely determining nor is it without any effect on man as an individual. Very much like the assumption of possibilism in geography, this assumption emphasizes that man, very much like David Matza's juvenile delinquent (1964), is in limbo. He is not always pushed into doing things. Most often he "drifts" into his action while actively considering other options available to him. You may recall that only the symbolic interactionist approach or the self theory in social psychology comes closest to this assumption. It is above all through this assumption that we can see the existence of reward and punishment in Islam which gives due emphasis to the "mitigating" circumstances, even in the commission of *Ḥarām* (prohibited acts or the taboos). Man is responsible for his own action but sometimes not quite so responsible.

These four assumptions together describe a sort of symbolic relationship between man and his social environment. It is on the basis of these assumptions that one may attempt a comprehensive theory of social behaviour as it unfolds in terms of organization and disorganization, deviance and conformity, marriage and divorce, war and peace, etc.

Research

Ba-Yunus and Ahmad's 'critical sociology ' (1983) falls in this category of Islamic social science. They call it critical because, as mentioned above, they envisaged Islamic sociological research mainly in terms of measuring the deviance of existing Muslim practices from Islamic ideal. There is little doubt that such a research strategy is long overdue. First, they have to develop an "ideal type" composed most probably of the salient features common to major schools of thought within Islam. Then, this ideal type is to be compared against the existing Muslim practice - at individual as well as collective level. For instance, one may be interested in the process of *Shūrā* (which is approximated by democracy in the sphere of political activity) and then try to see which Muslim state is closest to or farthest from it. Or, he may be interested in knowing which elements in Western democracy are convergent upon or divergent from Islamic *Shūrā*. Likewise, one may develop an ideal type of interestless banking and see which Muslim states have the capability of and are trying to institute this system in their economies and which are not, or one might be interested in the possibility of introducing this system in non-Muslim societies.

At the time we introduced that strategy, our theoretical views were still in an embryonic stage. Today, I find myself to be more confident about the theoretical assumption presented above. While critical research only produces data about *what*, it does not answer the question *why* or *how*. A research programme exploring the above theoretical assumption when articulated with critical research may yield information as to the degree and also the reason why Muslims have deviated from the Islamic ideal. Or, it may explore the question as to why non-Muslims have misgivings about Islam and Muslims. It is with the help of this kind of research that the Islamic social scientist, whether he be an economist, a sociologist, a historian, a political scientist or a psychologist, could develop strategies for the applied field.

Applied

Social analysis, as I mentioned before, has been and still is an integral part of the juristic activity among the Muslim *'ulamā'*, even if it has gone largely unrecognized on its own merit. The juristic discourse in Islam both oral and written, has been full of references to human nature, the state of the *ummah,* and lately the condition of non-Muslim, especially Western, societies as well. That much of this discussion is mainly in order to make a juristic point is quite apparent. However, that much of it is highly impressionistic and unauthenticated is also painfully apparent today. Humanity has become so complex that reliance on hearsay, impressions and simplistic over-generalizations about society would only lead to faulty Islamic legislation. If Islamic social sciences are to be of any help in this respect, Islamic law must become a part of the general scheme of the Islamic social science education. Traditionally, Islamic history has played this role quite successfully. There is no reason why other disciplines like economics, sociology, political science and even psychology cannot do that. Only when we accomplish this, can we speak of Muslim social scientists as being " the *'ulamā'* of the *ummah* today".

Preoccupation with reinterpreting and reforms in the Islamic law is not all that one can expect from Islamic social scientists. They are also expected to be and are growingly engaged in recommending institutional reforms at government levels. Khurshid Ahmad's Policy Studies Institute in Pakistan may to a great extent be credited with persuading the Pakistan government toward instituting *Zakāh* (the poor tax). Likewise, Nejatullah Siddiqui, a professor of economics from India, waged a long and almost lone fight for the establishment of interestless banking in Muslim countries. It seems that his dreams are only slowly coming true after all.

While it is much safer to call for reforms in the economic sphere of society, similar demands for, say, political reforms have a high possibility of being met with repressive measures on the part of Muslim governments, most of which, far from being Islamic, are not even democratic in their respective political structures. Ideally, Islamic political activity is based on the principle of *Shūrā* (consultation or mutual opinion seeking) which has to be based on *Taqwā* (piety) and be aimed at purely for the sake of the sovereignty of God alone (see Ba-Yunus and Ahmad, 1973;ch.5). In this case, the Islamic social scientist has not only to suggest ways and means as to how a political system could evolve toward *Shūrā,* he himself has to get involved in the movement towards this change, even if it calls for an open defiance of the government authority. There is no dearth of examples of such *'ulamā'* in the past - or in the present.

Conclusion

There are still two different kinds of educational systems in most Muslim countries - religious and secular. While most *'ulamā'* graduate from religious schools, most of those who went in pursuit of higher education in social science, graduate from secular colleges and universities. While most religious schools closed their doors to modern sciences, most secular schools only paid lip service to religious studies. If Islamic social science is to flourish, this dichotomy between the religious and the secular must go. Already some universities in the Muslim world have taken steps in this direction. The famous Al-Azhar of Egypt had already instituted such a programme which, after a brief setback during the socialist spell of the late president Jamal 'Abd al-Nasr, is reinstituted. The newly established Islamic university in Islamabad in Pakistan is following roughly the same philosophy, namely that the secular must be Islamized. Similar efforts are going on elsewhere. Islamization of education was the theme of the First World Conference on Muslim Education held at Makkah in the Spring of 1977. The Follow-up Committee of the said conference affiliated with the King Abdul Aziz University of Jeddah, collected, edited and published papers presented at that conference in several volumes which cover a wide variety of topics from natural and social sciences to arts. Likewise, the Association of Muslim Social Scientists, and the International Institute of Islamic Thought have similar objectives.

In short, there are signs that the efforts are underway to do away with the dichotomy of religious vs. secular education in Muslim countries. However, strange as it may sound, existing *'ulamā'* have generally remained outside the pale of these efforts by the "modernists". There is little doubt that in order for the above dichotomy to disappear, secular sciences have to be Islamized with heavy doses of the *Qur'ān* and *Sunnah* and other sources of the Islamic law and ethos. It is equally true that for the realization of this goal, traditional religious knowledge and its institutions have to be "modernized". This may be accomplished by a much wider spread of institutions like the Al-Azhar and the Islamic University of Islamabad.

Notes

Al-Faruqi, Ismail R., 1981a. Introduction to the Social Sciences section in, *Social and Natural Sciences: The Islamic Perspective.* Ismail R. Al-Faruqi and Abdullah O. Nasseef (eds). Hodder and Stoughton, U.K. and King Abdul Aziz University, Jeddah.

Al-Faruqi, Ismail R., 1981b. "Islamizing the Social Sciences" in, *Social and Natural Sciences: The Islamic Perspective.* Ismail R. Al-Faruqi and Abdullah O. Nasseef (eds). Hodder and Stoughton, U.K. and King Abdul Aziz University, Jeddah.

Ashraf, Syed Ali, 1981. Preface to the Social Science section in, *Social and Natural Sciences: The Islamic Perspective.* Ismail R. Al-Faruqi and Abdullah O. Nasseef (eds). Hodder and Stoughton, U.K. and King Abdul Aziz University, Jeddah.

Ba-Yunus, Ilyas, 1977. *Islam and Development* (ed.). The Association of Muslim Social Scientists. Plainfield, Indiana.

Ba-Yunus, Ilyas, 1981. "Sociology and Muslim Social Realities" in, *Social and Natural Sciences: The Islamic Perspective.* Ismail R. Al-Faruqi and Abdullah O. Nasseef (eds). Hodder and Stoughton, U.K. and King Abdul Aziz University, Jeddah.

Ba-Yunus, Ilyas and S. Farid Ahmad, 1985. *Islamic Sociology: An Introduction.* Hodder and Stoughton, U.K. and The Islamic Academy, U.K.

Esposito, John L., 1982. *Women in Muslim Family Law.* Syracuse University Press: Syracuse, New York.

Hoeble, E. Adamson, 1962. "Legal Dynamics in Pakistan" *American Anthropologist.*

Korson, Henry J., 1968. "Dower and Dowery as Indicators of Change in a Changing Muslim Society -Pakistan". *Journal of Marriage and the Family.*

Marsh, Robert W., 1967. *Comparative Sociology.* Harcourt, Brace and World, New York.

Matza, David, 1964. *Delinquency and Drift.* John Wiley , New York.

Merton, Robert K., 1973. "The Perspective of Insiders and Outsiders", in Robert K. Merton (ed.) *The Sociology of Science: Theoretical and Empirical Investigations.* University of Chicago Press, Chicago, Illinois.

Moltoch, H. and M. Lester, 1975. "Accidental News: The Great Oil Spill as Local Occurrence and National Event." *American Journal of Sociology.* 81:235-260.

Siddiqui, A. H., 1981. "An Islamic Concept of History" in, *Social and Natural Sciences: The Islamic Perspective.* Ismail R. Al-Faruqi and Abdullah O. Naseef (eds). Hodder and Stoughton and King Abdul Aziz University, Jeddah.

Siddiqui, K, 1981. "Beyond the Muslim Nation States" in, *Social and Natural Sciences: The Islamic Perspective.* Ismail R. Al-Faruqi and Abdullah O. Nasseef (eds). Hodder and Stoughton, U.K. and King Abdul Aziz University, Jeddah.

Siddiqui, M. N., 1981a. "Restructuring the Study of Economics in Muslim Universities" in, *Social and Natural Sciences: The Islamic Perspective.* Ismail R. Al-Faruqi and Abdullah O. Nasseef (eds). Hodder and Stoughton, U.K. and King Abdul Aziz University, Jeddah.

Siddiqui, M. N., 1981b. *Muslim Economic Thinking: A Survey of Contemporary Literature.* International Center for Islamic Economic Research, Jeddah and the Islamic Foundation, Leicester U.K..

Said, Edward, 1978. *Orientalism.* Vintage Books, New York.

Shariati, Ali, 1979. *On the Sociology of Islam.* Lectures Edited by Hamid Algar (Mizan Press, Berkeley).

Turner, Bryan S., 1974. *Weber and Islam.* Routledge and Kegan Paul, London.

Vander Zanden, James W., 1979. *Sociology.* John Wiley, New York.

127

Education, Religion and Social Science:
A Christian Approach

Graham Howes

I am genuinely uncertain as to where or how to begin. Perhaps with the prophet Moses, not only because he stands at the intersection between the two religious traditions that underpin this lecture series, but also becuase he has a fair claim to be called the world's first social scientist. As the Book of Numbers tells us, 'The Lord spoke to Moses in the Wilderness of Sinai, in the tent of meeting, saying 'take a census of all the congregations of the people of Israel, by families, by fathers' houses, according to the number of names'.[1]

But instead I have opted for some lines of W.H. Auden's (as much a Christian American as an American Christian) which he intoned before a Harvard audience - 'Thou Shalt not sit with statisticians nor commit a Social Science'. [2]

He subtitled his poem 'a reactionary Tract for the Times'. Yet today, four decades later, a kind of folk demonology of the social sciences still lingers on among both educators and many of the educated - from Dewey to Sir Keith Joseph as it were.

I do not want to dwell overlong on the components of that demonology, but in ascending order of seriousness they might include the following propositions:-

a) That the whole social science is a giant confidence trick, the most splendid 'lifemanship' ploy of all time, with social scientists as the Western academic equivalent of the trickster figure to be found in many African tribal societies.

128

b) That much social science, if impressive, is intellectually trivial - usually emphasising the quantitative at the expense of the qualitative, and adding up to little more than the systematic statement of the obvious. Indeed many sociologists (among whom I number myself) often find themselves impaled upon a kind of twentieth century version of Cardinal Morton's fork - if people agree with our findings they are obvious, if they disgree with them, they are wrong.

c) The social sciences are a kind of secular heresy, of American or dubious continental parentage which threatens to dilute, diminish and take over the more 'traditional' values of historiography, literature or education. The content is usually perceived as left wing - not creeping socialism, but creeping social scientism which is also socialism.

d) Finally, like all heresies it assumes not only a prophetic role about the destiny of society, but also a spurious universal competence for dealing with the ills of social man. The prophetic mantle is now worn by Habermas rather than Matthew Arnold, by Marcuse rather than Tawney.

Even such a popular demonology as this - although not so dissimilar, of course, to that found, for example, in Imperial reactions to early Christianity itself - must not be allowed to mask a more substantive set of objections to the *concepts* as well as the techniques and truth claims of the social sciences. Such objections are indeed largely encapsulated in the background rubric for this lecture course which I received earlier this academic year. In it reference is made to the 'secular concepts' of the social sciences which have 'revolutionised people's ideas about society and its mode of development' and have 'brought about uncertainty and insecurity '.

Let us identify these apparently corrosive *secular concepts* more closely. They are invoked in most working definitions of the social sciences, such as 'all activities which are concerned systematically to investigate and explain in aspects of the relationship between the individual and the society of which he is a part. Each social science chooses to abstract from the complex processes of social life, different relations between events and to approach the study of them using different methods!' Or if you prefer brevity 'the scientific study of man in relation to the society of which he is a part'.

Now implied in both definitions are four apparently secular concepts. They can be described as 'scientism', 'positivism', 'classification' and 'reductionism'. By 'scientism' I mean simply that there is a predominant commitment to scientific method. As Quentin Gibson puts it 'the features of abstraction, generality, reliance on empirical evidence, ethical neutrality and objectivity, the defining characteristics of science, *do* apply to the social sciences, and there are no viable alternatives'. Why? Because the job of social science is the job of any science, the discovery of predictable causal relationships. This means that social scientists now give allegiance to certain scientific assumptions. The first of these is that human behaviour is governed by psychological and social laws rather than being erratic or accidental, or divinely pre-ordained. Once this premise is accepted it opens the door to the study of causation in behaviour. This in turn leads to the assumption that when behaviour is understood it becomes susceptible to change by consciously directed processes.

It is further assumed that it is possible for the laws of human behaviour to be discovered and understood with constantly improving fullness and exactness through such scientific methods as observation, comparison, inference, hypothesising, classifying, generalizing, testing, and validating.

A second secular concept - not itself, as is often presumed, a necessary corollary of the adoption of the scientific method I have just outlined - is the commitment of the social sciences to positivism. There are three core components of this. One is the doctrine that knowledge must be based exclusively upon the methods of discoveries of science. The second is the assumption that all the social sciences should rest on a belief that there are regularities in social life which may be observed and which have causes which may be discovered, just as there are regularities in the physical world which may be observed and which are the concern of the so-called physical sciences. Thirdly in its methodology it requires that all areas of experience which are not susceptible to scientific observation and measurement be excluded from the field of enquiry: the emphasis is upon the quantifiable; thus what cannot be quantified - beliefs, values, etc - must be rigorously excluded.

Positivism is by no means extinct. I expect some of you will know the not entirely apocryphal story of the statistically minded American social scientist who not long ago, visited one of the best known social research centres in this country. Afterwards he was clearly puzzled, remarking 'when I asked for their data all they could give me was findings. When I asked for their findings all they could give me was anecdotes. And,' he added as a solemn afterthought, 'even the anecdotes were not classified'.

Which brings me neatly to the third secular concept encapsulated in the theory and method of the social sciences, and that is the process of *classification* or as it is sometimes more critically described, categorization. In so doing are we not, the argument runs, destroying individuality, denying the uniqueness of the individual and distorting reality when we place a person in a social category? Stereotyping is likely to occur when we form in our minds a composite picture of a given classification and confuse that composite picture with the live person whose behaviour places him or her in that classification. Then in truth injustice is done to that individual. Put differently (and I draw here upon Kurt Lewin's[3] well known distinction between Aristotelian and Galilean modes of thought) the more a classification merely puts together the superficial, outward manifestations of behaviour, the less useful it will be. The more it succeeds in putting together behaviour that springs from similar causative factors and similar dynamics the more useful it will be. In any case, behaviour is a continuum. In the strict sense of the word no arbitrary boundary can be set up between two closely related classifications; each merges into the next. Classification is a convenient device for breaking down our total knowledge into manageable units, but classification must be used with full recognition of its relationship to the continuous nature of differences between people and with full awareness of the individuality of the specific person and the degree to which his or her behaviour falls within a category.

The fourth secular attribute is that of *reductionism*. There is nothing novel in this, nor is it confined to the social sciences. You may recall how in the seventeenth century, Clarendon accused Thomas Hobbes of 'seeking to impose abstract, geometrical models'[4] on society. Yet by the mid-eighteenth century the emergence of Montesqieu's sociology marks, in Raymond Aron's phrase 'a moment in man's reflection on historical reality, the moment when the concept of the social, of society, becomes the centre of interest, replacing the concept of politics, or of the regime of the State.[5] And while Montesqieu still regarded politics as in some measure an autonomous activity, both Compte (the founding father of positivism) and Marx, a century later, made it wholly dependent on, or a reflection of, other social forces. Indeed social scientific thought largely arose out of an attempt to grasp the complex consequences of industrial and political revolution and to extend these to societies other than eighteenth and nineteenth century Europe. The price of this widening of the angle of the lense was - and still is - a social science that may coarsen rather than refine our view of the historical process.

One implication of the argument outlined above is that these four concepts and methods within the social sciences are not only intrinsically secular but also have a secularizing effect upon the norms and values of other institutions. I was careful to say 'the argument outlined' rather than 'as I have argued'. For it is not in fact *my* argument at all. My own argument runs, instead, along three distinct axes.

One is to suggest that most of the social sciences are now in a 'post-classical' phase where the primacy of the secular concepts I have referred to have been either powerfully refined or successfully challenged and dethroned. To begin with, most social scientists today are highly sensitized to the philosophical issues attendant upon the use of the so-called scientific method in their work. We are well aware that assumptions of lawfulness and of cause and effect relationships in behaviour can lead to a crudely over-determined view of man. We do not of course take the libertarian stand that each human action is completely free and unaffected by previous character, life history, current experience, nor do we believe that all choice, all behaviour is the determined, necessary, and inflexible result of previously existing physical or environmental causes. Rather we believe that there exists a measure of freedom influenced by constitutional factors, previous life experiences and the current environment. Through the scientific method we hope to understand these latter factors and then to modify them or to use them in the pursuit of individual and social goals. The concept of lawfulness excludes the possibility of freedom and spontaneity in behaviour only when lawfulness is considered synonymous with exact repetition and frequency.

Hence many of us have become increasingly critical of those of our colleagues who go on making insistent and rather shrill demands that we strengthen the 'scientific' element in the social sciences, without giving any careful consideration to the manner in which these 'sciences' can be made more scientific. It is indeed a prime example of what they themselves label 'cultural lag' that so many social scientists still seek to adopt the model of Victorian physics as their prototype of science, oblivious that the claims of modern science to an understanding of universal truth, eternally valid in the objective facts of nature, are much more hesitant and much more qualified than they were a century ago. My impression is that although there may still be a type of science composed of classificatory statements, such as the determination of the genus and species of plants and animals, this is now regarded as being comparatively old-fashioned. The developing end of science, where the interesting work is done and the reputations are made, is to be found in the amplification and consolidation of evolutionary theory, rather than in the collection of what may be regarded by some as 'incontrovertible' facts or raw data.

Among social scientists, as John Rex[6] has put it, 'it is now widely recognized that the arguments of empirical science can never have the same sort of certainty as the rational demonstrations of deductive logic do. Science is not thought of as the search for a set of final and absolute truths. Rather it is seen as an always relatively imperfect and incomplete attempt to explain and predict the events which we experience'. In this sense the search for absolute truth is without hope. In any case it is a philosophical commonplace that empirical truth (ultimately) rests upon certain presuppositions or *a priori* truths, so that absolute objectivity cannot be achieved.

Above all, the modern philosophical concern with language has shown how the social scientist's ideas of reality, no less than the layman's are given to him by the language he uses. Wittgenstein was foremost in showing how the concepts we have determine the *form* of the experience we have of the world. He writes 'that the world is *my* world

134

shows itself in the fact that the limits of my language (of the only langage I can undrstand) means the limit of *my* world'.[7] Thus all observation is in terms of a conceptual framework, and the facts which one elicits are of course in the last analysis sense data perceived in terms of concepts.

It is unsurprising therefore that many of today's social scientists are beating a fairly hasty retreat from classical positivism - the doctrine that knowledge must be based exclusively upon the methods and discoveries of science. To use scientific methods to establish what can in fact be learned by those methods does not necessarily commit one to the belief that this is the only source of knowledge. As it is, most of us are uncomfortably (or perhaps comfortably) aware that Comte's nineteenth century prediction about the future of our craft (i.e. 'with the inevitable growth of rational societies .... the logic of science and technology would find a parallel expression in the social sciences')[8] simply hasn't happened. Instead, most of us have begged, borrowed or stolen from such areas as phenomenology, linguistics and structural anthropology to steer a relatively straight course between positivist and intuitionist claims. That is to say as a social scientist one cannot be a thoroughgoing positivist because events in the human world are in a sense unique. Yet causal explanations have some validity and the search for laws of human behaviour and social phenomena is largely justified. Conceptually and technically we have moved in from the extremities of positivism towards what Robert Merton has called 'theories of the middle range'. We have come to recognize the existence of a set of low probability rules of human interaction in terms of which we can make tentative explanations of the past, comment accurately on the present, and modestly predict the future. Similarly few of us are now prepared to reduce or classify human social life in exclusively macro-historical terms. For as C. Wright Mills once wrote of Talcott Parsons 'the nerve of the grand

at religious services, self-identification as Protestant, Catholic, or Jew, acceptance of specified elementary religious beliefs, etc.) which are quite different from each other. He then distinguished five 'core dimensions of religiosity' in which he believed the religious commitment of any person in any religion may be manifested. (1) The *ritualistic* dimension is that of religious *practices* - what people who are religious do in the external expression of their religion. It includes church attendance, confessing, praying, fasting, tithing, working for the church, etc. (2) The *ideological* dimension deals with what religious people *believe*. These beliefs are of several kinds (purposive, warranting, and implementing). Unbelief similarly appears in several forms and is a valid subject for religious research. (3) The *intellectual* or cognitive dimension is concerned with what people *know* about their religion, church, sacred scriptures, etc. (4) The *experiential* dimension focuses around what people feel. Religious emotions, sensations, and perceptions related to God, ultimate reality, participation in religious activities, and personal or group religious experiences belong in this category. (5) The *consequential* dimension pertains to the *effects* of the religious rituals, beliefs, knowledge, and experiences and hence is on a different level of conceptual abstraction. It is the area of "works" in contrast to "faith" in the Christian theological sense.

His basic purpose was to promote empirical sophistication in religious research, so he elaborated each of these dimensions, pointing out how various aspects of them are researchable and stressing the interaction of each dimension with all the others. He also expressed a belief which I believe to be too optimistic; he wrote that "within one or another of these dimensions all of the many and diverse manifestations of religiosity prescribed by the different religions of the world can be ordered". If the word "all" is taken literally, then since all of the five dimensions are researchable, the totality of the manifestations of any and all religions, including those elements which are believed to be "supernatural" and "spiritual", eventually are subject to "scientific analysis".

Now many sociologists, like many theologians or believers, are apt to feel uneasy when Glock's five dimensions are presented as a summary of the totality of the Christian religion. The missing element is difficult to identify, but it might be labelled as the realm of faith, revelation, illumination and insight which some have called 'the sacred', 'the holy', or 'the spiritual'. From the perspective of Christian values each of these dimensions is an inadequate basis for a satisfactory analysis of religious life. All five are of great importance, of course, but there is a missing factor. The factor is sometimes more than a combination or blend of all five dimensions; it is the total man-God and God-man relationship. Measuring each of the other dimensions is not identical with measuring religious faith, ultimate concern or existential commitment. Hence some sociologists, in their critique of Glock's approach, postulate that there is a sixth dimension of religiosity which may be tentatively labelled the 'transcendental', or 'existential' or 'spiritual'. It is not parallel to the other five but runs completely through them and colours them all. It is the very essence of religious life, what David Mobery [12] has labelled 'the true life'. For him 'the supernatural is not made a separate section of social life, something juxtaposed to the natural, which individuals may accept or reject at will. In studying society in its complex wholeness, in the concrete, it is found to exist within the atmosphere of the supernatural'. The natural and the supernatural order meet in man. Even he who denies the supernatural root and branch of the religious life in his search for purely natural explanations of religion is involved with a 'sociology of the supernatural' in a negative sense.

With this example fresh in our minds let me return once again to Professor Ashraf's original rubric, where he asks 'what sort of formulation of religious concepts would be necessary in the social sciences if secularist concepts are to be replaced'. But I hope I have managed to show you that in the social sciences, especially in the Western Christian tradition, 'secular' and 'religious' concepts are *not* in conflict or tension: they are not even, in my view, in uneasy juxtaposition. Instead they are achieving 'increasingly' a kind of mutual elision. This is most marked in three areas. One is a new found awareness of both the limitations of the social sciences in explaining human problems of motive and value, and of the deterministic error which can occur when a statement on the social origins and conditions of an idea, belief or phenomenon is held to imply an answer to the question of its value or validity. Secondly, in suggesting, as social scientists do, that man's social nature may be his most fundamental attribute, they are raising questions of traditional and otherwise theological concern. In what sense is man a social animal? In what sense do we belong to society? In what sense does society belong to us? What is the nature of our dependence upon it? How shall we interpret the unity of the whole to which our individual lives are bound? These questions are aspects of one fundamental question - the relation of the unit, the individual to the group and to the social system. This question is the starting point and the focus of all social scientific investigation, and, to a great extent, the fruitfulness of any study in this field is measured by its contribution to the problem of the relationship between the individual and society, and of the nature of Man himself.

Thirdly, and especially pertinent to the overall context of these lectures, is whether or not the social sciences present any distinct challenge to Christian morality. Here one finds oneself basically rehearsing most of the old familiar arguments.

For example, 'should we do what God says because what He says is good, or is it because God says it, it is therefore good? If the first is the case then presumably there are criteria apart from God which make it good and if these are to be found in a social science one is not challenging a religious faith particularly. If the second case holds then social science is hardly in a position to challenge God with respect to an absolute morality.

That said, however, morality is concerned with how people live together and the real challenge to religious people that the social sciences can offer is to open their eyes to the context within which they try to live their lives and achieve their valued goals (on this earth). There are severe limitations to the realization of Utopia but these are not perhaps so limiting when we have knowledge of them as when we are in ignorance of their existence. Social science can for example warn us of likely unintended consequences and make us more aware of the structural constraints which impede - or could facilitate - the implementation of chosen ends. An all too obvious example springs to mind when one considers the role of legal, political, religious, scientific and bureaucratic institutions in the implementation of aid to Third World countries. There is another, related, challenge which is neatly summed up in the opening paragraph of Reinhold Niebuhr's *Moral Man and Immoral Society* ... a sharp distinction must be drawn between the moral and social behaviour of individuals and of social groups, national, racial, and economic; and.... this distinction justifies and necessitates political policies which a purely individualistic ethic must always find embarrassing. [13]

What has been suggested throughout this lecture is that the social sciences cannot challenge any ontological theological reality. They can however throw down a gauntlet to those religions which hold a 'Many are the Keys...' theology. As for the kind of religious faith which is exclusive in providing its own description of the world, the gauntlet will not be picked up but the social sciences may raise a sceptical eyebrow in its direction.

Notes

1. *Numbers* XIV 27-9.
2. W.H. Auden: 'Unto this Lyre' in *Nones,* Faber 1948.
3. Kurt Lewin: 'The Conflict between Aristotelian and Galilean modes of thought' in *Contemporary Physchology* XIX 1954.
4. Cited in Brian Wormald: *Clarendon,* C.U.P. 1958 p.192.
5. Raymond Aron: Main Currents in Sociological Thought Vol. I, Penguin 1960 p.67.
6. John Rex: *Key Problems of Sociological Theory,* Routledge 1961 p.30.
7. L. Wittgenstein: *Philosophical Investigations,* Blackwell 1953 p.171.
8. Cited in G. Hawthorn: *Enlightenment and Despair,* C.U.P. 1976 p.48.
9. C. Wright Mills: *The Sociological Imagination,* Oxford 1959 p.49-50.
10. See especially P. Glasner: *The Sociology of Secularization,* Routledge 1977 Passim.
11. In *Religious Education* Vol. 57 No.4 1962.
12. D. Mobery in *Social Compass* XVII No. 2. 1969.
13. R. Niebuhr: *Moral Man and Immoral Society,* Harvard U.P. 1948 vi.

Islamic Education and Moral Development

Syed Ali Ashraf

Morality and religion are not segregated into two distinctive units in Islam. One cannot be religious and immoral at the same time. The moral norm is set by the Qur'ān and the Sunnah of the Prophet Muhammad, peace be on him, hence to do something immoral would mean violating the God-given norm and hence committing a sin. Though the norm is set by God and exemplified by the Prophet, each individual is endowed with complete freedom to choose to follow the norm or ignore it. It is this freedom of choice which turns human action into a moral or an immoral action because this freedom compels the individual to choose, and choice is determined by certain factors which may or may not be morally justifiable.

This moral justification involves the objective realisation of the rightness or wrongness of the factors that compel an individual to make a certain choice and engage in a certain action. Rightness and Wrongness can be determined only on the basis of how far the choice and the resultant action help the moral development of the person and lead her or him towards a more and more comprehensive and balanced growth of the total personality or how far choice and action can further injustice and do harm to the individual and damage the personality. "Balanced growth" also implies the recognition of certain faculties within each individual: The Spirit, the Intellect, the Intelligence, Imagination and the Senses. The senses pertain to the body, but they become humanly active and generate feelings and emotive response only when another factor that is not the direct product of this physical body, gives power to the eyes

142

to see, the ears to hear, the mind to think, and something intangible to intuit. When that intangible something leaves the body, though the matter or material components of the body remain, it cannot see, hear, speak or think or intuit. That something is not material energy. The dead body like dead wood has material energy - each atom retains that energy. But the power to make the dead walk and talk and think is something else. This is the work of the Spirit of a human being.

This Spirit is endowed with moral perception. This is evident even in very young children. If you were to slap a two year old child who can speak, how would the child respond? It would protest, 'Why have you slapped me?' 'What have I done wrong?' The child may not use those exact words, but its response will indicate that it has an innate sense of justice, of right and wrong, and it is this sense that demands an explanation of this behaviour from someone who has treated the child badly. Similarly the love of Truth is ingrained in every soul. That is why even though a father is strict but fulfils what he promises to the child, the child trusts him more than another person, say, the uncle, who shows his affection profusely but never fulfils his promise. Even though the child may fictionalise and love to make up tales, its innate love of Truth and mistrust for untruth becomes manifest in the child's response. The same thing is true of a child's response to love and hatred, beauty and ugliness, generosity and miserliness. Who taught the child how to respond? No one in this world. It is innate. Only some one who can endow the Spirit with this sensibility can claim to have bestowed these values within the Spirit.

From the Qur'ān we learn that God has endowed human beings with these values. They are innate in the human Spirit. Our common sense also convinces us, as shown above, that this value-consciousness is innate in the human Spirit. Thus our findings only corroborate that religious conviction has a justifiable basis. The Spiritual entity in a human being cannot therefore be considered as a social product, it is an inherent reality. As this reality is not an individually unique thing, as every single human being has basically the same spiritual consciousness with intellect, imagination, intelligence and feelings and the same innate consciousness of supreme values such as Truth and Justice, this spiritual consciousness with ingrained values cannot but be the product of the impingement of a Supreme being on the material self of the human being. This is what is meant by the Qur'ān when it says that after making the body of Adam God breathed into him Spirit from His own Spirit (Qur'ān: 15:29). Morality is thus not a social product but an innate reality.

The Qur'ān gives a further explanation to it which guides us to focus our attention on its metaphysical and spiritual dimension. It says that God showed Adam, the first man, His Trust which He had shown to the hills and the skies and they had refused to accept it for fear that they would not be able to preserve and maintain it. After creating Adam God showed the Trust to him. The Spirit granted to Adam had given him the power to assess his own ability and he accepted the Trust (Qur'ān: 33:72).

Different interpreters of the Qur'ān have given different meanings of this 'Trust'. From my own reading it appears that this 'Trust' is the knowledge of the essence of every created thing. According to the Qur'ān Man at first knew nothing but God "taught Man what he did not know', (Qur'ān: 96:5). This infusion of knowledge obviously refers to the knowledge granted to the first human being, Adam. The Qur'ān tells us that after creating Adam and infusing his material body with Spirit from God's own Spirit he was taught the 'names' of every created object. As the Qur'ānic verse regarding the acceptance of the 'Trust' by Adam, as explained by the Prophet, indicates that Adam was shown the 'Trust' immediately after the Spirit had entered his body, this 'Trust' could not be anything but the 'Names of everything' that God taught him. It was after Adam consented to accept the 'Trust' that God taught him the 'Names'. (Qur'ān 2:31)

The 'name' of any object rouses in our mind the idea about the object. It is not the colour or shape or size that comes first to our mind, it is the essence of the object, 'table', 'sun', 'Man', 'horse', all these words immediately mean what they are in essence. Teaching Adam the 'Names' of everything therefore means making Adam conscious of the essence of every single created object.

As God creates, He uses one or other of His Qualities to bring everything into existence. Thus in everything in the creation is the reflection of one or the other of His Qualities. His Beauty, Grandeur, Creativity, Destructive power, Peace, Mercy, all these are reflected in His creation. By stating, further, that after creating everything in six days, He established Himself on His Throne which, according to the Qur'ān, embraces the entire creation, it is stressed that God's authority is holding the entire creation together in a systematic pattern which allows birth and death, change and destruction and creation. Thus the entire creation came into existence because God Willed it. It is retaining its system, order and birth, growth and death, because God's Will is ever active allowing the entire creation to unfold gradually. Thus creation is in 'essence' already complete but He brings it into the material form according to a set pattern. Hence the essence of each object lies both in the Quality with the help of which He has brought that object into essential existence and in the Will which helps both the primal creation and the gradual material unfolding.

It is the knowledge of this essence that was given to Adam. He could acquire this knowledge only when God endowed him with understanding that God's Qualities are reflected in creation. One can understand the Qualities only when one possesses them. Therefore God's own Qualities are reflected in the 'self' of Adam so that he could

145

understand the essence of this creation and its relationship with the creator. This 'endowment' is the 'Trust' (*amānah*)

Creation is an expression and reflection of God's Qualities and accepting the reflection of God's Qualities within one's 'self' also implies accepting the duty of preserving the system ordained by God. Thus the acceptance of the 'Trust' means the acceptance of the duty of honouring the 'Trust' by honouring the 'Names' of God reflected in creation. These two are interlinked. God would not have granted the reflection of His Qualities within the human 'self' had not Adam accepted the condition of preserving them, honouring them and maintaining them in the entire creation and within himself. This is the explanation we get in the interpretation of the Qur'ānic verse regarding the 'Trust' in a saying *(hadīth)* of the Prophet. This interpretation is logical. How can a person understand and preserve the Qualities of God in the creation if that person does not care to understand and preserve them within one's own self. It is only with the recognition, growth and development of full awareness of these Qualities within one's own self that one gains the ability, power and strength to preserve and maintain them in the universe as a whole.

This is where the whole moral structure of the 'Being' and 'becoming' of the human personality become manifest and the relationship between that structure and the need for faith in God become understandable.

The entire creation reflects millions of Qualities and powers of God. The ninety-nine 'Names' of God that the Qur'ān and the Hadith of the Prophet speak of makes us aware of those essential basic Qualities which provide the foundation of all the Qualities and the total structure of Reality as reflected in the creation. These Qualities such as Justice, Truth, Love, Mercy, Creativity, Destruction - all these provide the human being with the Knowledge of the essence of the norm to ascertain Truth, dispense justice, show love and mercy, maintain creativity and allow destruction.

The difference between God's having these Qualities and a human being's realisation of these qualities within the inner 'self' lies in the nature of these qualities. In the case of God they are from God and are Absolutes. In the case of a human being, they are a gift from God already implanted within the soul. They are reflections of the Absolutes. They need nurture and a norm to nurture by whereas in the case of God they are His Qualities which are at His disposal.

People need a moral structure in society and a definite tradition of ethical norms based on certain assumptions regarding human nature in order to cultivate the moral sensibility, allow the different moral imperatives to flourish and the balanced growth of the self to be accomplished. This structure religion provides through faith. Moreover, besides these qualities that lie hidden within the human self there is another aspect of this self which has a negative effect on the human personality. The body being a composition of all the aspects of what may be generally termed as *matter*, the material self of human beings demand the satisfaction of material, this-worldly and selfish interests. That aspect of the human self uses passions, anger and logic to attain selfish ends if not by force then by arguments, or by rousing emotions through appeal to narrow self interests. It is a well known fact that uncontrolled anger results in violence and fights; uncontrolled sexual behaviour leads to the breakdown of a peaceful home; uncontrolled greed leads to violence, cheating and hypocrisy. But when someone exercises control over these very passions and desires, that person can use these passions for survival and growth as a balanced personality. Some sense of anger is necessary to protect ourselves and to stand up to injustice. Sexual passion is necessary for bringing children into the world, for joy, health; and good family life teaches us how to love, and develop selflessness through the give and take of life within a family.

This control comes from a person's innate sense of justice, selfless love and love of truth, but these qualities always need a norm, an example for justification to one's own self and a deep love for that example. The conflict between selfishness and selflessness, between desires and passions on the one side and justice and control on the other is so acute in all human beings that it is only this deep spiritual love for the supreme example of selfless self-sacrifice that emotionally 'purifies' a human soul and the person gets ready to sacrifice all material interests for the sake of vindicating, preserving and furthering truth, justice and love.

The prophetic model is posited as the ideal model for human beings. For a Muslim all prophets are presented in the Qur'ān as providing the ideal norm because even though they were liable to make mistakes, they never committed a sin. For Muslims Prophet Muhammad, peace be upon him, is the best human norm, *Uswah ḥasanah*, according to the Qur'ān. One way of teaching that concept was then and even now is indoctrination, both in traditional schools and at home. Children get accustomed to this norm because the prophetic *Sunnah* and the fundamental beliefs provide the unquestioned assumptions regarding faith in God, revelations, human nature and all values and codes of behaviour. The Prophet unites the moral and the godly. Though the Qur'ān is the basic source, as his life is the human embodiment of the Qur'ān, all human life is regarded in Islam as the endeavour to emulate his ways and be like him. Religion/Morality dichotomy is thus denied. The Qualities of God are most perfectly reflected in his nature, hence he provides for his followers the model method of uniting the Divine and the earthly, and of preserving and promoting the Divine order in nature and humanity through the preservation and promotion of those Divine qualities in the individual and society according to the system granted by God in the Qur'ān and exemplified by the Prophet. This system provides what is known as *adab* (etiquette). Education is therefore explained as *ta'dīb*, which is the Arabic word for 'culture' and 'the training of moral sensibility through the teaching of etiquette'. Thus the Qur'ān gives moral/religious principles which are applied and implemented at the human level by the prophetic practices or the Sunnah.

The Qur'ān and the Sunnah thus provide Muslims with a compendium and source of moral truth which has a definitive and interpretable dimension. Thus education means not merely to study them but to apply them to individual and social life. The text and its study not only make children aware of moral and religious truth, they also have an instrumental dimension, namely, that they could lead to moral/religious practice.

There is also a notion of intentionality in the Qur'ān and the Sunnah. God is not blind or capricious. He has created human beings with the specific object of becoming true worshippers of God. And, as explained earlier, Adam's choice of accepting the Trust indicates the true nature of the worshipper and the possibility of becoming God's viceregent provided people exercise free will to know the truth about themselves and choose to follow the prescribed path. This knowing the truth has a further dimension besides the one about God's Qualities mentioned earlier. It means also knowing the pre-natal covenant between all human souls and God, that God alone can be worshipped. Thus 'classical' or 'traditional' education serves the dual purpose of making the individual conscious of this commitment and covenant, and also of freedom of choice and the prophetic model for the individual's choice. By reading the Qur'ān one comes to know the pre-natal covenant and the ingrained nature of the qualities and understands the interrelationship between them. By examining one's own self one realises the truth of the Qur'ānic concept of qualities within one's own self and also feels that an individual has the freedom to accept that truth or reject it.

From the time of the Prophet there have been discussions about free will and fate. These questions need to be answered in order to appreciate the nature of human freedom. First we must understand whether Adam's acceptance of the Trust limits our choice or not. Second, in what way pre-natal acceptance of the covenant affects and limits post-natal freedom. Third, if one is fated to be in haven or hell is one compelled to act according to a set pattern or is one free to choose?

Adam's acceptance of the Trust meant two things. It meant first that the human self became enriched with the reflection of God's Qualities which is the source of all moral good in human beings and the possibility of the human being reaching the status of God's viceregency on this earth. In other words it not only enriches the 'being' but also gave it the possibility of supremacy under God in the entire creation. Secondly, it was the acceptance of the Trust that made God grant the human being *freedom* to choose, a quality which nature does not possess nor do the animals. Animals behave instinctively, nature behaves according to set laws, 'willingly' or 'unwillingly' as the Qur'ān puts it. It is only the human being who has been granted the freedom of choice, freedom of knowing one's self, one's responsibilities, one's duties, one's future possibilities and the freedom to act. Thus Adam's acceptance of the Trust does limit human nature to a basic pattern that necessitates the following of a definite norm that is suitable and appropriate for the preservation, maintenance and expression of those qualities. But at the same time it grants the human being the freedom to choose or reject the norm. In other words the study of the Qur'ān and the Sunnah should make us aware of our true nature and the norm needed for its proper growth and development as a moral being.

As regards the pre-natal covenant between God and

human souls, it does not limit human freedom, it only means God implanted within the human soul the consciousness that only by submitting one's will completely and whole-heartedly to the Will of God can a human being get the pleasure of knowing the true nature of oneself and of fulfilling the Trust and becoming the viceregent of God on earth. The choice of knowing or not knowing, of becoming or not becoming conscious of the Trust, of accepting the norm given in principle by God and exemplified by the Prophet still remain the choice of the individual concerned. This covenant further implies that just as the human being is composed of the dual nature of the 'spiritual' and the 'physical', it has two souls *(nafsān)* , the higher rational soul *(al-nafs al-nāṭiqah)* and the lower animal soul *(al-nafs al-ḥayawāniyyah)*. God proclaimed His sovereignty to the rational soul, hence the rational soul knows God as its true Lord *(rabb)* and the true Object of Worship *(ilāh)* (Qur'ān 7:172;3:18). But the human being forgets this covenant *(mīthāq, 'ahd)* because it is also composed of forgetfulness *(nisyān)*. Hence education through the study of the texts with faith should enable the rational soul to assert its supremacy and confirm and affirm the covenant within the total self of the human being so that the total self is able to accept the guidance *(hudā)* granted by God and fulfil the Trust through action *('amal)* and thereby perform the job of worshipping God (the job of *'ibādah*) (Qur'ān 31:56). Establishment of pre-natal covenant is therefore to instil into the rational soul the Knowledge of God-human being relationship so that through education in the post-natal period that knowledge is revealed to the self from within. The rational soul then frees itself from forgetfulness and subjugation to the animal self and exercises its freedom by using its power *(quwwah)* and capacity *(wus')* to fulfil its Trust and thereby do justice *('adl)* to itself.

The rational soul is thus in constant conflict with the animal self and with the Satanic forces prevalent in the world, the forces that have been characterised in the Qur'ān as the most cruel enemy of the humankind. When the rational self is almost lulled to sleep and the human being forgets its covenant, it disobyes the instructions of God and thus makes a wrong choice, and does harm to itself (*zulm*). By doing *zulm* to itself it does injustice to itself. Justice demands that the rational soul should get the authority vested on it by God so that it can fulfil the Trust accepted by it and through its good deeds (*'amal*) allow the soul to draw nearer to God and become His *khalīfah*. By making wrong choice, the animal self is usurping the place reserved for the rational soul and is thus guilty of doing injustice. That is why God says that He does not do injustice and harm to the human being; it is the human being who does harm and injustice to itself. (*Qur'ān* 4:123; 10.44).

This implies that the human being must become aware of its covenant with God, and know the truth about its real nature so that it does not break its covenant, misuse its energies, deviate from its real nature and hence from the path of justice to itself. The Qur'ān and the Sunnah provide that knowledge and also make the human being aware of the limits within which it should act, the norm it should follow, the spiritual gain that inevitably is reaped through just action, the loss that one suffers when one does injustice to oneself by violating that norm. The stress thus is always on the result of one's action on one's inner self.

The other aspect of this moral consciousness generated through this knowledge is that it is not dry-as-just logic alone that would make a true human being. Heart is fully involved in this process, hence only that person is said to be a true *mu'min* (faithful person) who loves God and the Prophet more than himself, his family, tribe or entire humanity. It is this love that gives the joy of the fulfilment of the covenant and saves a person from acting mechanically. That mechanical action can become cruel whereas this love leads to human considerations when one is acting

152

according to Shari'ah.

According to the traditional educational system, therefore, it is necessary to cultivate faith in order to get the hidden qualities manifested so that the human personality has a balanced growth and the human being becomes a 'moral' being and follows the prophetic norm. The best means always adopted to attain this end is to generate love and reverence for the prophets, especially for Prophet Muhammad, peace and blessings of God be upon them all, through the study of Qur'ānic tales of the prophets, the detailed biography of Prophet Muhammad, peace be upon him, and the life history of the Companions of the Prophet. The intention is not only to teach the pupils the facts of history but also and primarily, to convince them of the tremendous impact of faith on the personality of those very people who as adversaries were ready to kill the Prophet but became totally transformed through faith. As a result the cruel barbaric pagan Arabs turned into a revolutionary force of moral-spiritual-cultural transformation of human society. This means that sincere acceptance of faith affects the human heart and thereby allows the Spirit in which lies embedded the basic qualities granted by God to influence and direct the intellect to engage actively towards the establishment, maintenance and furtherance of the balanced order in individuals and societies. Primary emphasis in moral education, thus, is on the *purification* of the heart through faith. The Qur'ān says:

> Have they never journeyed through the land so that they may have hearts to reason with, or ears to hear with? It is not the eyes, but the hearts in the breasts that are blind (22:46).

The Prophet says the same thing in the following Hadith:

> Listen, there is a piece of flesh in the human body, if it is pure, the whole body remains pure. And when it

is perverted the whole body becomes perverted. And
that is the heart.

The Prophetic statement establishes an intimate
relationship between the body and the soul, matter and
spiritual purity, integrity and acumen, good and evil, morality
and spirituality. Heart is the cognitive-affective spiritual
organ spiritually inherent in some way within the bodily
heart of the individual. In Arabic both the physical heart
and the spiritual organ are termed as *qalb*. The Qur'ān, the
Word of God, is described as something that 'descended'
on the *qalb* of the Prophet. Thus sensations, passions,
desires generated in the heart that materially affect the
personality can be purified of selfishness when the heart is
'illumined' by faith and the heart starts loving the 'good' by
following the example of the 'good'.

That is why in traditional education the teacher plays the
role that the Prophet played in the community. Love and
reverence for the teacher are generated within the heart if
the teacher is 'good' both in thought and feelings that
come spontaneously from the person and in the activities
that are governed and guided by the 'good'. It is a common
sense reality that whenever and wherever a person sees the
'good' in the form of selfless love, charity, righteousness,
truthfulness, sincerity, justice, mercy and care for all creation,
balanced and impartial judgment, humility, then his or her
heart is immediately attracted towards that manifestation,
and love and reverence are generated within the heart for
the person whose behaviour reflects those qualities. To be
a moral person is much more than intellectually stating
moral principles after a cut and dried dry-as-dust assessment.
To be moral is to be a *whole* human being who lives and acts
in the world and in whom the head and the heart work in
coordination and love for the good is manifest through *good
deeds.*

The Islamic ethic is thus intimately related to a practical

manifestation. A Muslim is asked to take a leap in action as well as in thought and feelings. Even if the thinking capacity cannot penetrate beyond the external layers of the thinking mind, the feelings must be right, hence one's motivations, intentions and understanding must be controlled by the heart. That is why the Prophet said, "Actions will be judged by intentions". At the same time moral principles must be expressed through moral actions which spell out the moral life-style. Knowledge of the moral principles are important but the manifestation of morality in action is more important both individually and in the community. That is why Islamic ethics are formulated in specific laws, practices, parables and stories which are all aimed at daily practice and behaviour. As without a knowledge of these laws and without a love for the good, to ensure which these laws are formulated in the Qur'ān and Sunnah, it is almost impossible to know the norm and act accordingly. The study of these basics are necessary. This is what Ghazali meant when he described this knowledge as *farḍ 'ayn* (obligatory) for all Muslims. Thus this ethic is both cognitive and affective, but the crucial arena is action described in the Qur'ān and the Sunnah as *'amal*. Hence the study or knowledge of the Qur'ān, Sunnah, Sīrah (life of the Prophet), early history, rules and laws *(fiqh)* and such other ancillary subjects are important because of the vital impact on right action.

This study is expected to make Muslim children conscious of another crucial dimension of the Islamic ethic - it is both collective and individualistic. A Muslim must be conscious of his or her duty towards the Muslim ummah (global community). This ummatic consciousness is immanent in the society. A Muslim will be considered to have failed in his or her duty if he/she remains ignorant of the responsibility to the rest of the Muslim community of the world. The godly way is rooted in the collective tradition and context.

Islamic Approach vis-a-vis the Secularist Approach to Moral Education

Islamic education, in essence, is thus primarily character-education in the sense of education for the 'good' life, education that would help pupils to gain internal awareness of the Reality in order to be able to develop a moral life-style, a maturity and a behavioural system which would reflect the life of the Qur'ān and Sunnah. Thus internalisation of the 'good', making the 'good' a part of one's being and thereby enabling the good to become manifest by doing the 'good' are far more important in this education system than moral deliberations about God for the sake of clarifying one's moral feelings and beliefs which predominate in the secular modern western system of education.

The difference between moral education within the secular system and moral education within the Islamic system are thus basically deep. Islamic moral education is concerned with the acquisition of knowledge about and acceptance of a very definitive life-style and behavioural pattern. But in a secular education system moral development is seen in terms first of patterns of moral thinking which, it is expected, leads to moral actions. The former is principled-behavioural and the other is cognitive-developmental.

Moreover, in the secular system, morality and moral education should operate independent of prior religious assumptions. In Islamic education moral education is intrinsically bound to religious assumptions.

Secular education allows that moral reasoning may lead to faith, though this is not considered as inevitable, and therefore faith is not considered as integral to moral development. In the case of Islamic education faith is integrally necessary for moral development of the total self.

The content plays an important role in moral education in the Islamic way of thinking. The very act of studying the

Qur'ān and the Sunnah even in the form of stories or incidents and situations from them is regarded in the Islamic system as performing a moral deed. When a pupil approaches them from faith and reverence a person is emotionally and spiritually affected enough to make the moral choice. In the secularist system the study of conflicting theories based on multi-dimensional and often contrary approaches is encouraged. Hence there is a lack of a norm of judgement and a neutral approach is encouraged even though the teacher may be religious in personal convictions.

In the Islamic education, especially in the traditional schools of thought, there is no psychological theory of moral development. There is the theory of conflict between, and the tension related to 'good-inclinations' and 'bad-inclinations.' There is no linear growth of morality. There is a complex inter-relationship between cognition, attitudes, behaviours, norms, community-life and backsliding.

There are some similarities between the two systems as regards moral education. First, both systems consider such education as an individual thing. Each child must be treated individually. Second, both systems consider the school, its setting, its curricular and extra-curricular activities, teacher-student interaction, student activities and student environment as relevant factors in the moral development of the child. Third, both systems reject the notion that the child can become moral through inculcation of moral laws. The secularists consider moral thinking, and Islamic education considers moral life as the essence of moral education. In both however, intention and motivation are regarded as relevant factors. Fourth, both systems originate from universal principles: the secularist system in the humanist ideals and the Islamic system in the ideal human model in the Prophet. Fifth, both systems assume that study must lead to moral action. Intellectual and action sphere should not be segregated. Unfortunately much of science education gives priority to amoral research, and much

Moral And Religious Education:

A Christian Approach

John E. Greer

Patrick Shea, a Roman Catholic civil servant who became Permanent secretary of the Northern Ireland Ministry of Education in 1969, tells in his autobiography *Voices and the Sound of Drums* how he rose to this position from his humble beginnings. His account of his primary education and of the Principal of Deerpark National School, Athlone, in the early 1920s makes interesting reading. "He had a ferocious temper, a liberal mind, the talents of a circus clown and a vast knowledge of greyhound coursing, horse-racing and boxing .... On the wall behind him hung a large rectangular display card with, on the one side, in heavy black letters, the words 'SECULAR INSTRUCTION' and on the other 'RELIGIOUS INSTRUCTION'. The finger-worn stains on the bottom corners of the card bore witness to his puncti-liousness in ensuring that, as required by the rules of the Commissioners of National Education, the exposed side truly conveyed what was going on in the school."[1] The principal may have had few problems distinguishing secu-lar from religious instruction and knowing when to turn the card to one side or the other. However, the matter is far from simple. Is religious instruction so easily distinguished from secular instruction? To change the question closer to the subject of this chapter, are what we today call religious education and secular education, of which moral educa-tion is an integral part, discrete and separate aspects of the curriculum?

The Relationship of Religion and Morality

The case is commonly argued today for the autonomy of morality, that man's moral understanding is not necessarily dependent on or inseparable from his religious beliefs.[2] It is not our intention to get embroiled in philosophical arguments about this complex issue and the connection or lack of connection between the language of morality and the language of religion.

We wish simply to draw attention to the fact that for many religious believers moral knowledge is firmly rooted in religious knowledge. The integral relationship of religion and morality is asserted, for example, by Leszek Kolakowski who quotes Plotinus, "God, if you talk about him without true virtue, is only a name."[3] In his study of religion, Kolakowski claims "that there is a special kind of perception characteristic of the realm of the sacred. In this realm the moral and the cognitive aspects of the act of perception are so blended that they are indistinguishable from each other: only an analysis "from outside" produces this distinction. A believer does not receive religious teaching in the form of mythical tales or theoretical statements, out of which he subsequently proceeds to normative conclusions. The moral content is given directly in the very act of perceiving and understanding, for this act merges with moral committment." Religion for Kolakowski is "the realm of worship wherein understanding, knowledge, the feeling of participation in the ultimate reality (whether or not a personal God is meant) and moral commitment appear as a single act, whose subsequent segregation into separate classes of metaphysical, moral and other assertions might be useful but is bound to distort the sense of the original act of worship."[4] There are of course different possible relationships between religion and morality, but if morality is integral to ultimate vision, then scholars who stand apart and who look in from the outside at a religious tradition and speak of the 'ethical dimension'[5] or the 'consequential dimension'[6] are making a distinction which distorts the meaning of religion at the same time as it tries to facilitate its academic study.

Christian Theology and Morality

What Kolakowski claims concerning religion in general certainly appears to be true of the specific religion with which we are concerned, the Christian faith. To theologian and believer alike, Christian moral teaching is closely dependent upon and related to Christian theology. For example the Christian scholar James Gustafson has recently argued that ethics must be theocentric because the whole of the Christian religion is a response to the power of God; "ethics are ethics in the theocentric perspective."[7] The same point was made by a scientist, Evelyn Ebsworth, Professor of Molecular Chemistry in the University of Edinburgh, in a televised interview with Ronald Eyre. "Our lives are related to the lives of one another and they are related through God and through Christ .... All the moral imperatives that I know are derived from my faith."[8] Similarly Mother Teresa has justified her work in Calcutta and elsewhere by her Christian faith. "I can't bear the pain when people call me a social worker. My life is devoted to Christ; it is for him that I breathe and see. Had I been a social worker I'd have left it long ago."[9]

We turn now to examine in more detail why it can be argued that "moral life belongs to the *essence* of the Christian faith,"[10] why it is consistently held that Christian faith and morality belong together so closely and so firmly. Expressed most simply, Christian morality emerged as a response to the revelation of God as Father, Son and Spirit. The central belief of the Jewish tradition is that God is a personal moral being who has taken the initiative in making himself known to men as righteous and loving. According to T.W. Manson, "in Hebrew ethics the governing factor is the relation of human persons to a Divine Person; and that means that the good is not so much the object of philosophical enquiry as the content of divine revelation. '*He has shown* thee, O man, what is good; and what doth *the Lord require* of thee but to do justly and to love mercy and to walk humbly with thy God?' (Micah 6.8). The emphasis is on God and the things revealed by him; it is a matter of acceptance and obedience. The relation between God and the single living corporate body called Israel is a covenant relation. The terms of the covenant are the commands given and the promises made by God." [11] In practice, the law provided a system of rules covering the life of the Jew from cradle to grave, and "its deficiencies as a guide to the whole of life were made good by the rabbanic casuistry, resulting in a mass of writings known as the Halakah."[12] The Christian tradition inherited and transformed Hebrew ethics and the Hebrew covenant, and added to the Old Testament Canon what became the New Testament Canon of sacred writings. Christianity, like Judaism, was from the start "a religion which was indissolubly linked with an ethic …. In one way or another, belief about God was the source of principles of conduct."[13] But in adding the gospels, epistles and other books, Jesus, rather than the law, was the centre of revelation. While the teaching of Jesus was given a place of honour and authority it did not provide detailed instructions for behaviour. Instead it focused on the principle of love (Mark12[31FF]; Matthew 22[39F]; Luke 6[27]) and it proclaimed the nature of God's Kingdom to stimulate those who heard to think for themselves and to make their own response. "Which of these three, do you think, proved neighbour to the man who fell among the robbers?" (Luke10[36]) Jesus was the originator of the Christian movement, and the tradition of his teaching was passed on faithfully in the Church community and eventually crytallised out in the four Gospels, but his teaching and the

Church's understanding of his teaching became so merged that scholars now find it difficult to separate the one form the other. Today "we cannot be sure whether teaching ascribed to Jesus in the Gospels, written twenty to fifty years after Paul's letters, is his own or arose in the early Church."[14] This should not be a surprise to us since the early Church did not treat Jesus' teaching as an all-encompassing set of regulations for life but looked to the Spirit of God for guidance (1 Cor. 7[40]), particularly where no teaching of Jesus was available. Like the earliest Christians, Christians today do not find precise answers to their moral problems in the ethical teaching of the New Testament. The Christian writings speak of the gracious relationship with himself which God has given through Christ. "To be Christian is at root to share that style of relationship with God which Jesus initiated. What then are its implications for moral life, for our relationships with our fellows, friends and opponents?"[15] With these words Holden raises the crucial question facing the Christian today. In answering the question, it must be remembered that Christian moralising is not absent from the 19 centuries since the end of the New Testament period. There is a long tradition of moral reflection expressed in the Roman Catholic tradition in papal pronouncements and in the magisterium of the Church, and also expressed, in Anglican and Protestant moral teaching. This tradition of moral reflection safeguards against arbitrariness or individualism. For as J.H. Oldham has put it, "The God to whom we are called to respond is not capricious but constant in His dealing with men. In each new situation in which men find themselves His will can be learned only in the light of His will already revealed in Christ, in the Bible and in the experience of the Church"[16] It may be added that while there is much in the christian moral tradition which is distinctively Christian and reflects the Christians theology from which it sprang, Christian moralists have often shared much in common with their non-Christian contemporaries. The beginnings of this may be seen in the pages of the New Testament itself where St. Paul and the author of the pastoral epistles made use of pagan lists of virtues and vices and of catalogues of households duties. (e.g. Colossians 3[18FF], Ephesians 5[22FF], Titus 1[10], 2Timothy 2[16])[17]

Christian morality has a trinitarian basis [18] since it is the response of faith to the God of Israel, to the Father of Jesus and to the Spirit of the risen Lord. "At the centre of Christian morality is an affirmation of the initiating, accompanying and fulfilling love of God."[19] What about the third theological virtue, hope? Hope is important as an attitude which supplies a dynamic to moral and social efforts. According to John Macquarrie, "hope that there is at least a chance of success seems to be indispensable to any human striving, but hope, in turn, rests on deep convictions about the universe in which human life is lived."[20] This hope is the eschatological confidence that moral effort does attain, "that human history and likewise the whole cosmic process, of which our history is a small part, do have a goal and a directedness. They move, however painfully and – it would seem – uncertainly, towards a consummation, in which that striving after the good in which man engages and in which he may believe himself to be supported by the activity of God himself is increasingly brought to fruition ... eschatological hope holds out the promise that what is now achieved only fitfully and ambiguously will eventually be manifested in its fullness."[21] Thus we may see that hope plays an indispensable role in its underpinning of Christian morality through its encouragement of moral effort.

This account of Christian morality and its relationships to Christian theology is based upon the work of contemporary Christian scholars who use the methods of Biblical criticism. Their approach to Christian ethics is very different from that of moralists in pre-critical times or of fundamentalists in the contemporary world. It takes seriously the cultural context of Jesus and the movement which emerged from his death and resurrection. It also takes seriously the cultural context of Christians living today and so it provides a more helpful and realistic guide to the handling of the complex moral problems wich are faced by scientists, politicians, businessmen, lawyers, medical workers and educators in the world of the end of the twentieth century. No longer can texts be picked out of the Bible and applied in a simplistic authoritarian way in totally different contexts to today's profound personal and social questions. Christian theology expressed in contemporary terms can thus provide Christians with guidance in Christian ethics, "the art of distinguishing right form wrong in the business of Christian living."[22] Examples of this new critical approach in action may be seen in recent reports sponsored by the Church of England Board of Social Responsibility, such as, *Marriage and the Church's Task*[23], *Homosexual Relationships*[24] and *The Church and the Bomb*.[25]

Christian morality is clearly a morality of response to God, known as Father, Son and Spirit. It thus follows that Christian religious education must not isolate the doctrinal and the moral dimensions of the faith but handle both dimensions together as it initiates people of any age into an intelligent informed understanding of their faith. Persons being so educated must be free to rspond as they learn about Jesus, the Kingdom he proclaims, the moral demands he makes and the community of faith which he has initiated. But are people of all ages able to make such a response? The growth of faith is a subject which is too large and too complex for this chapter. For an account of research into faith development we refer to the work of James Fowler.[26] At this point we turn to examine the process of moral development to find out what may be learned about moral education as it relates to Christian doctrine.

Moral Development

In the last 50 years, a number of psychologists have studied the development of moral judgement from childhood to adolescence. Accounts of this research are readily available, for example, in *Moral Development: A Guide to Piaget and Kohlberg* by Duska and Whelan[27] and *Promoting Moral Growth: From Piaget to Kohlberg* by Hersh, Paolitto and Reimer.[28] Very briefly, in 1932 Piaget found two stages in moral development, heteronomy and autonomy.[29] In 1958 Kohlberg investigated moral reasoning more fully and discovered six stages at three levels:

Pre-conventional level
(1) Obedience and punishment orientations
(2) Naively egotistic orientation

Conventional level
(3) Orientation to approval and pleasing others
(4) Authority and social-order maintaining orientation

Post-conventional level
(5) Contractual legalistic orientation
(6) Conscience or principle orientation

More recently, Kohlberg has dropped the sixth stage which he failed to find in American and Turkish longitudinal data, and which he concluded "was mainly a theoretical construction suggested by the writings of "elite" figures like Martin Luther King, not an empirically confirmed developmental construct."[30] He now views the construct of

166

a sixth stage as an elaboration of an advanced substage of Stage 5. The most recent critical evaluation of Kohlberg's research has been carried out by Bergling[31] who tested the central postulates of the theory, that the six stages of moral development form an invariant sequence or succession, and that this invariant sequence is universal, early stages being necessary prerequisites for later ones. Bergling found that the evidence he examined did not support the invariant sequence postulate nor the universality postulate. Though there were more progressive than regressive changes in moral development for stages 1 to 4, subjects at stages 4 to 6 were more likely to regress or remain fixated. Progressive changes in moral development occured stepwise for children in stages 1 to 3 but not necessarily for adolescents or adults at the higher stages. Bergling also found that the same set of stages was not present in all countries. In some, stage 6 was absent, in others stages 4, 5 and 6 were lacking, while in Nigeria stage 3 was under-represented. Bergling's reputation of the universality postulate has caused him to oppose the purely cognitive-developmental interpretation of the development of moral reasoning, and to recognise the importance of cultural influences stemming from the religious values of the society. "From stage 1 to stage 4 instruction can rely upon a cognitive-developmental process to account for an important part of the cahnges in moral reasoning. Beginning with stage 5, however, an ideological motivation seems to be necessary in choosing the content of instruction on moral issues."[32]

What does this recent assessment of Kohlberg's theory mean for moral educators? While the moral development process may be less clear-cut and stage-like than once thought, stages 1 to 5 do provide a useful model for moral educators. They form a convenient structure which can be used to conceptualise how Christians develop in their grasp of and reasoning about moral issues, particularly as these issues are related to religious doctrine. According to Duska and Whelan "over and above the fact that a person's particular religious beliefs and affiliations provide content for the structures that Kohlberg has identified, it is also the case that the structures act as a filter through which these beliefs and affiliations must pass. In such a passing the beliefs and perceptions of the affiliations will be modified."[33] Thus as children grow up, they achieve a more adequate grasp of moral issues as they are attracted beyond, for examples the fear of punishment in hell, to selfish hopes of reward in heaven, to maintaining the approval of teachers, parents and clergy, to unquestioning obedience to the Church, and finally to the autonomy of mature Christian commitment. The task of moral education, then, is to help children, adolescents and adults to reflect on their stage of moral reasoning and to attempt to stimulate higher cognitive levels, remembering that individuals seem to be attracted to reasoning one stage higher than their predominant stage. The aim of the Christian moral educator is to help pupils to reach stage 5 where they are able to respond to the central Christian principle of love as experienced from God the Father, as incarnated in Jesus, and as embodied in the contemporary life and witness of the Christian community. So we see a fit or match between the content of Christian morality as expressed by modern scholarships (Bergling's ideological instruction) and the structure of moral development as expressed by cognitive psychologists.

Implicit in this cognitive developmental scheme is the notion that the highest and the most adequate form of moral reasoning is stage 5 when the law and order imposed by State or Church is subject to scrutiny and questioning for which formal operational thinking is necessary. This questioning may give rise to conflicts over authority, particularly if the Church to which a person belongs is one with a distinctive moral stand on issues such as premarital sexual intercourse and abortion. The Roman Catholic Church has recently faced this problem in the Pastoral Constitution on the Church in the Modern World of the Second Vatican Council and has come to accept, in theory at any rate, the importance of human freedom. "Only in freedom can man direct himself towards goodness. Our contemporaries make much of this freedom and pursue it eagerly; and rightly so, to be sure. Often, however, they foster it perversely as a license for doing whatever pleases them, even if it is evil."

For its part, authentic freedom is an exceptional sign of the divine image within man. For God has willed that man be left "in the hand of his own counsel" so that he can seek his Creator spontaneously, and come freely to utter and blissful perfection through loyalty to Him. Hence man's dignity demands that he acts according to a knowing and free choice. Such a choice is personally motivated and prompted from within. It does not result from blind internal impulse nor from mere external pressure."[34] In his discussion of the education of conscience, Kevin Nichols echoes these words when he argues that "at the heart of the gospel there is a reverence for personal freedom, for the inner autonomy of a decision made in the light of values as a necessary element in true human goodness."[35] Paradoxically, however, "Autonomy may well be a characteristic of moral life involving the acceptance of an existing code, even a strict one. A life can be rationally self-directive yet lean heavily on the traditional moral wisdom of the Church."[36] So what might appear on the surface to be stage 4 morality might in fact be stage 5.

In this Chapter, we have outlined Christian morality in relation to theology and the cognitive developmental approach to moral development, and we have seen the fit between the content provided by the first and the structure provided by the second. Before leaving this subject, we wish to note briefly how this cognitive developmental approach to moral education differs from some others. It differs, for

169

example, from the social skills approach to moral education of the School Council Project on moral education
where "the main motive for treating others with consideration is ... because such behavior is pleasing in itself and
can be rewarding"[37] which would seem to be a good example of moral education based firmly on stage 2. It also differs
from the "secular morality" approach of Downey and Kelly
who dismiss any morality based on religion as authoritarian
in essence, (presumably stage 4) and who argue "that over
the centuries religion and theology have inhibited rather
than enhanced moral debate, since they have focused
attention on questions of the interpretation of the Word of
God rather than on how man could set about thinking for
himself on moral issues." This linking of morality to religion is unacceptable "because it denies to the individual the
right to choose his own beliefs, moral principles and behaviour on his own terms and in the light of his own
thinking." It is also "unacceptable because it does not allow
for the evolution of moral knowledge or understanding....
Our moral understanding must be such as to enable us to
adjust to changing social circumstances, to meet new moral
problems and modify our principles to deal with them.
This is not possible with a morality that is based on authority."[38] Downey and Kelly write with the best of intentions
but with little understanding of how Christian moral education can meet the moral challenges of today in a way that
respects the developmental stage of the pupil and at the
same time attempts to help children mature through the
stages of development to achieve autonomy based on the
Christian concept of love.

This chapter has not been concerned with the practice of
Christian religious and moral education but with its theory.
It has not been concerned with the setting in which this
education takes place nor with the agents who are responsible for organising it, parents, teachers, clergy etc. It
has assumed that such education *is* education and not some

form of conditioning or indoctrination. It has taken for granted that the recipients share some measure of Christian faith and are struggling to grow to maturity in that faith. Only in passing has it defended the concept of Christian moral education against attacks by those who argue for the autonomy of morals and the desirability of secular morality. The importance of Christian moral and religious education being integrated together in the curriculum has been stated rather than argued in detail. These tasks need to be taken up and pursued further by other Christian educators.

Two Exemplars

To round off our argument we would like to put some flesh on our theoretical bones and to point brief portraits of two Christians who live in the contemporary world, and who exemplify the Christian who practises his or her faith, Dr. Allan Boesak and Mrs. Rosemary Haughton. Both persons spoke at the 1983 Summerfest organised by the Corrymeela Community at Ballycastle in Northern Ireland, and the quotations are from their addresses at that Conference.

Allan Boesak [39]

Allan Boesak is a minister of the Nederduitse Gereformeede Sendingkirk (coloured) in South Africa, and in 1982 he was elected President of the World Alliance of Reformed Churches. Boesak speaks of the prophetic witness of the Church to the real challenges of the world and to the demands of the Kingdom of God. "This prophetic life is made possible by the Spirit of God and it is through the prophetic witness that the power of the Spirit that moves the Church is revealed. It is true that where the Spirit is there is freedom, not freedom to do as we please, not a freedom to take us away from this world, not a freedom in the sense that we are now free from the cares of this world, because being the Christian and believing in Jesus Christ does not make of us emigrants out of history. On the contrary it places us squarely within the turmoil of human history and the life of the world." So Boesak is moved by the Spirit to oppose detention without trail, to expose torture in prisons, to draw attention to the break-up of family life, to protest against the homelands system which strips people of their property and citizenship, and the Mixed Marriages Act which forbids different races marrying. He opposes the policies of the South African Government which, ironically, claims that the purpose of its policies and its constitution is to uphold Christian standards and which has created the oppressive system of apartheid as an expression of its belief in the Christian God. But claims Boesak, "people are not Christian just because they call themselves so,and the government is not Christian by decree and a country is not Christian because a government declares it so. People are Christians when they learn to respond to the demands of the gospel of Jesus Christ." "Reconciliation is never cheap. It cost Jesus Christ his life. What makes us think we can get away with less? The Church can only participate as God's witnessing people in the world, in God's act of reconciliation and forgiveness and the creation of peace if we are also willing to lay our lives on the line for that which is right and just and for love and for peace, and for the sake of the Kingdom of God." "Forgiveness cannot be done through the strength of human beings. It can only be done through the strength and the power of the Spirit of God." "But we can be sure that victory will come." So Boesak cares for his people and fights their oppressors through non-violent means. Faced with the power and wealth of the South African government, intimidated by threats of death and banning, he bears witness to his faith in impossible circumstances. He also exemplifies many of the themes we have been discussing in relationship to Christian morality and faith in God.

Rosemary Haughton [40]

Rosemary Haughton is a Roman Catholic theologian, the mother of ten children and the author of a number of books. She was a founder member of the Lothlorien Community, Kirkcudbrightshire and also of Wellspring House, Gloucester, Massachusetts, where she now spends most of her time. Both communities were set up as places of healing to which people could go for rest and support, and both for Rosemary Haughton were now expressions of the life of the Church. In her Scottish community she "began to see that the gathering of people in an apparently haphazard way could actually show all the signs of the ingathering of people called by the Spirit, even if they wouldn't use that kind of language themselves. And the kind of sense of what was going on in that group, of the sharing and the supporting and the courage and the hopefulness very much showed the spirit at work." The American community grew out of a parish in which a small ecumenical group decided to explore more deeply what it meant to be a Christian community, to be Christian on the move. The group acquired a house "a house of hospitality, it's a house where people in the area who are homeless or in crises can come for a while, to help to put themselves together, to get some sense of support, to see what their options are, to begin to make a few choices where many times they had felt no choices was possible, that they were finished. All kinds of people. Adolescents thrown out of their families, women who had suffered abuse in marriage and had finally realised that there was nothing they could do but leave, people who were recovering from alcoholism, people trying to get out of the drug scene, all kinds of people, of many different ages, have come to the house.... Everybody eats together, works together, tries to support the house." So the Wellspring community has launched its experiment in community, its discovery of what friendship could be, its exploration of a new style of mission and Christian witness.

We end our discussion of Christian moral and religious education with these two accounts of contemporary Christians. They illustrate in different ways, in different circumstances, the close relationship between morality and belief, the experiential and experimental nature of Christianity, the challenges and the difficulties which Christians face in making moral decisions in the real world of today. Allan and Rosemary live dangerously, even recklessly, and their style of discipleship of Jesus is challenging to those whose lives are lived in more quiet surroundings. Their moral decisions are not easily made with calm minds and reasoned arguments. As Rosemary said, "What it more often feels like in practice is that your life is turned upside down and made a mess of and you end up somewhere else after the explosion has died down and you wonder, where you have got to, and you try to do something with it." In both cases, God's poor and oppressed people are served in the power of the Spirit of Jesus. We might well wonder what sense the principal of Deerpark National School, Athlone would have made of it all and what side of the card would have been turned to the front if he had been doing lessons on the history if South Africa or the meeting of social needs by new Christian communities. To change the question to the subject of this chapter, would Christian educators today call such lessons Religious Education or Moral Education? To ask such a question is to draw attention to its absurdity.

Conclusion

In this chapter, we have outlined the responsive nature of Christian morality and we have indicated how the pattern of each person's response is influenced by the developmental process. We have shown the way in wich mature Christian morality involves the practice of the love ethic and we have exemplified this in the particular situations of Allan

Boesak and Rosemary Haughton. Thus the task of the Christian educator must not be to inculcate a static system of rules and regulations. Rather, to use Rahner's words, it must be to nurture each Christian who lives in the modern world in "the holy art of finding the concrete prescription for his own decision in the personal call of God, in other words the logic of concrete particular decision which of course does justice to eternal regulative principles."[41]

Notes

1. Shea, P. (1981) *Voices and the Sound of Drums*, Belfast, Blackstaff Press, p.16
2. Hirst, P.H. (1965) "Morals, Religion and the Maintained School", *British Journal of Educational Studies*, 14, pp. 5–18
3. Kolakowski, L. (1982) *Religion*, London: Fontana, p. 172
4. ibid p. 174–5
5. Smart, N. (1968) *Secular Eduction and the Logic of Religion*, London, Faber, p. 16
6. Glock, C.Y. and Stark, R. (1965) *Religion and Society in Tension*, Chicago, Rand McNally, p. 21
7. Gustafson, J.M. (1981) *Theology and Ethics*, Oxford, Balckwell, p. 342
8. Ebsworth, E. (1981) *God and the Scientist*, Interview with Ronald Eyre, B.B.C. Television, February 18, 1981
9. Quoted in "Superstar of India", *The Times*, August 4th 1983
10. Wogaman, J.P. (1976) *A Christian Method of Moral Judgement*, London, SCM Press, p. 62
11. Manson, T.W. (1960) *Ethics and the Gospel*, SCM Press, p.18
12. Linders, B. "The Bible and Christian Ethics" in Dunstan, G.R. (ed.) (1975) *Duty and Discernment*, SCM Press, p. 65
13. Houlden, J.L. (1975) *Ethics and the New Testament*, Mowbrays, p. 23
14. ibid p. 103
15. ibid p. 117
16. Oldham, J.H. quoted in Whyte, J. "Protestant Ethics and the Will of God", in Dunstan, G.R. (ed.) (1975) op. cit. p. 118
17. ibid pp. 64 and 93

18. Lehmann, P. (1976) *Ethics in a Christian Context*, Harper & Row p. 105

19. Baelz, P. (1977) *Ethics and Belief*, Sheldon Press, p. 111

20. Macquarrie, J. (1970) *Three Issues in Ethics*, SCM Press, p. 136

21. ibid p. 137

22. op. cit. p. 65

23. (1978) *Marriage and the Church's Task*, Church Information Office

24. (1979) *Homosexual Relationships*, Church Information Office

25. (1982) *The Church and the Bomb*, Church Information Office

26. Fowler, J.W. (1974) "Towards a Developmental Perspective on Faith", *Religious Education*, LXIX, March–April, p. 207–19

27. Duska, R. and Whelan, M. (1977) *Moral Development: A Guide to Piaget and Kohlberg*, Gill and Macmillan

28. Hersh, R.H., Paolitto, D.P. and Reimer, S. (1979) *Promoting Moral Growth*, Longman

29. Piaget, J. (1932) *The Moral Judgment of the Child*, Penguin edition 1977

30. Kohlberg, L. (1978) "Revisions in the Theory and Practice of Moral Development" in *New Directions for Child Development*, 2, p. 86

31. Bergling, K. (1981) *Moral development: the Validity of Kohlberg's Theory*, Almqvist and Wiksell International

32. ibid. p. 86

33. Duska, R. and Whelan, M. op. cit. p. 83

34. Abbott, W.M. (1966) ed. *The Documents of Vatican II*, Chapman, p. 214

35. Nichols, K. (1979) *Orientations*, S. Paul Publications, p. 57

36. ibid. p. 59

37. McPhail, P., Ungoed-Thomas, J.R. and Chapman, H. (1972), *Moral Education in the Secondary School*, Longman, p. 66

38. Downey, M. and Kelly, A.V. (1978) *Moral Education Theory and Practice*, Harper and Row, p. 7

39. For an account of his liberation theology and liberation ethics see Boesak, A.A. (1978) *Black Theology, Black Power*, Mowbrays

40. For an example of her theology of experience and its moral consequences see Haughton, P. (1972) *The Knife Edge of Experience*, Darton, Longman and Todd

41. Rahner, K. Quoted in Nichols, K. op. cit. p. 65

British Muslims and the Maintained Schools

Mohammad Akram Khan-Cheema

I Muslims in Britain

The families of most Muslims now permanently settled in Britain emigrated from different parts of the world and this has resulted in a wide variety of socio-cultural heritages within the Muslim Community. What is often overlooked is a very interesting historical presence of a small but very devout and energetic group of Muslims with an Anglo-Saxon heritage. Turks, Greeks (both from Cyprus and the mainlands), Pakistanis, Nigerians, Yemenis, Indians, Moroccans, Libyans, Saudi Arabians, Bengalis, Ghanians, Sri Lankans, Malaysians, Palestinians, Lebanese, Afghans, Egyptians, Sudanese, Polish, Ukranians, Chinese, Africans of Asian origin and Asians of Caribbean origins and virtually every other nationality in the world form a part of that Muslim Community in Britain.

This has either proved to be an exciting and positively beneficial variety for those who have used it as an opportunity to evolve a deeper appreciation of the global nature of the Muslim Ummah[1] and the universal message of Islam which transcends all barriers; or else it has been seen as a source of 'problems' by others. The important point here is to realise that the Muslims in Britain do not form a homogeneous community with one socio-linguistic heritage. It is equally important to say that we form an ideologically united Ummah under the universal banner of Islam.

II Islamic Education

The Unity of Muslims can best be nourished by an education through the medium of Arabic (the language of the Holy Qur'ān); and an Islamic way of life (*Dīn*) can best be maintained through an education system which considers a thorough knowledge and understanding of the Qur'ān and Sunnah[2] as its 'core curriculum'. This is so comprehensive and interdependent that it covers all aspects of human life and all our various needs. If the message of Islam is understood in the way that great Muslim Philosophers like Al-Ghazzali[3] explained it, then it would not be seen as a temporary system that fits into a specific historical period, nor would it be a local system set up for merely a certain generation or a particular environment. Islam is not the minimum rites of worship that believers collectively or individually perform to achieve a modicum of faith. It is not limited to being a guide on the path to Paradise either. It is certainly not a subject of great academic interest related to the five pillars of Islam and beautifully exotic places of worship which display artistic excellence of a particular period in our history.

Faith is the central point of Islamic education and the Islamic code. As presented by the Qur'ān, faith is not merely a word to be uttered and then forgotten as a person goes about his/her diverse practical worldly affairs. Faith is the pivot around which all life turns: the conscience, the intellect and the practical sense all alike, so that if knowledge, skills and values are seen as the basic aims of education, the main priority must be given to values. The knowledge would fall into two categories: That which is 'Divine' (Qur'ānic), and all other knowledge.

The Qur'ān is the constitution revealed by Allah to regulate and govern human life, therefore any skills taught must also be in accordance with the Qur'ānic guidance.

The Qur'ān and Sunnah together provide the practical

code for regulating human life in its noblest form and in all its spheres political, economic, social, intellectual and moral; that is, a life which is befitting to human beings whom Allah has ennobled and raised above all that He has created.

Islam is meant to be an internal regulator of behaviour, aiding the individual in his/her judgement, choice and in establishing a conscience. Self control and self discipline come from being always aware of Allah (what I like to call walking with God). Most authors (Muslims and non-Muslims) have expressed this as either a 'fear of God' or a 'complete submission to the Will of God'. I feel both these expressions in the English language can be and have been misunderstood. Muslims are then made out to be fatalists or believers in a God who is devoid of love, mercy and compassion. Islam, as I understand it, does not require that there be no self renewal of society. As the essential nature of human beings does not change, all human societies, man made or otherwise, are essentially based on a central core of principles and values which remain intact. We respond to each new environmental situation with a new precise response, formulated from the similarities and differences between the present situation and our past experience (Hadith) and internalise the new information from the present event in a form usable for evaluating and responding to future events (Shari'ah⁴). This is what the study of Sunnah and Shari'ah inculcates into the life of a Muslim.

It is therefore not too difficult to imagine if a whole tradition of anti-Islamic thinking were to be eradicated from the British cultural heritage (as I acknowledge is being done very slowly in some quarters in recent years) then the contribution of Islam could well complement the exciting process of continuous re-evaluation and improvement in the development of an education for our contemporary pluralist society. However the fact remains that the British education system sees the presence of Muslims as a 'problem' and some of the Muslims unfortunately con-

other relevant Community Languages from the school curriculum, adequate concern about single sex provision either as separate schools or within co-educational schools and an absence of a balanced 'cultural' content in the curriculum. I feel however that Black[6] organisations will continue to distrust the state schools and will continue to feel frustrated even if our schools try to meet some of these requirements until they feel that they have some considerable involvement in the decision making machinery and have some control, power or authority over their children's educational diet. 'Madrasas' are here to stay in order to meet particular needs and give the faith communities a sense of self fulfilment. There are grave doubts expressed by almost everyone about the nature of supplementary provision in most 'Madrasas'. It may be said that they meet the needs of ritualistic self identity and are serving a purpose almost as a protest but one doubts whether the majority of present supplementary schools come anywhere near meeting the spiritual and actual fulfilment of our Muslim children. There are a few notable exceptions. Most parents, however, seem to be dissatisfied with the present provision and consider the 'Madrasa' to be far from ideal; but improvements will come with experience, time and better resources. The commitment towards this ideal is unquestionable.

It is inevitable that because of the absence of an enlightened form of an Islamic perspective in the recent mainstream historical development of the 'British culture' whenever there is a discussion about the education of Muslims in the state schools it tends to be 'problems' orientated. It is also true to say that religion of any kind is no longer the measure of social or political dynamics within our secular society.

British Muslims in facing up to the challenge of such an 'alien' environment and trying to create links with the social, cultural, political and administrative structures are invariably trapped into talking about 'problems'.

The Local Education Authorities (LEAs) concentrate on the 'problems' they face in catering for the needs of their Muslim pupils. More often than not these 'problems' are associated with the adult Muslim community because the schools are less likely to have any 'problems' with their young Muslim pupils. It is also not unusual to hear of 'their' social disadvantage (in the inner city areas or deprived areas), 'their' illiteracy, 'their' rural/peasant background and sometimes of 'their' lack of concern for the education of 'their' children. Non attendance at school parents meetings is often interpreted as a measure of apathy or lack of interest in 'their' children's education. Some headteachers who are actively engaged in pressurising their LEA's into providing better facilities and resources when faced with this sort of 'apathy' or apparent lack of support from the Muslim parents become extremely frustrated and disheartened. They invariably end up asking.....

Why are they so submissive?
Why don't they fight for their legitimate rights?
Why don't they question the Authorities about Institutional racism.....?
Why dont't they demand that something be done about the underachievement of their children?
Why don't they fight against the racial harrassment and the overt racialism?
Why don't they fight against the cuts in resources?...etc

The general image of Islam as presented by the media at the international level in Iran, in Pakistan, Saudi Arabia, Iraq, Egypt, Palestine during the Arab-Israeli conflict, Lebanon, Afghanistan, Libya etc is problem orientated and full of 'illogical' conflicts, isn't it? This perpetuates negative stereotypes and creates enormous barriers which militate against some of the splendid efforts towards harmony and mutual appreciation. It succeeded in poisoning the minds of British Muslims, particularly the younger generation, making them less assertive of their faith commitment, until, that is, the "Rushdie" affair and the Gulf crisis. Young British Muslims have now found a new perspective and are less inclined to be intimidated by those in 'authority' and by those who feel they hold 'power' positions.

IV The 'Problems'

Some of the problems which appear on our agenda concerning the education of our Muslim children in our state schools are not unique to the Muslims alone. For example many parents are concerned about the influence of a permissive society or the effects of institutional and cultural 'racism' on the children who are unable to take full advantage of the education provided without feeling oppressed and harassed. One hears objections about 'sex education' in the school curriculum on the grounds of the type of content or the attitude of the teachers (and/or schools) who offer this subject or the age range at which it is offered. Others express concern about the effect of conflicting values and norms expected in school, at home and within the peer group. It is alleged that the disciplines and 'standard' of behaviour accepted in schools is falling. The 'standard' of academic achievement is also dropping and therefore our schools are 'failing' our children. Some Muslims might say that the reason for all this is the lack of proper Islamic values but others suggest a number of different reasons e.g., comprehensivisation, too much liberal and woolly thinking, or leftist trendy teachers etc.

In the context of providing an enlightened form of 'good' education within a pluralist society what the 'Swann'[7] report calls "Education for All", there has been an effective and increasingly strong opinion that the changes that have taken place have been too few and fall far short of the ideal.

There is a long way to go before the principles of "Education for All" are accepted, even longer before they are implemented and realised nationally.

Proposed changes in the form of Multifaith (Agreed Syllabi according to some recent interpretations of the 1944 Education Act) curriculum were considered as tokenistic prior to the 1988 Education Reform Act, but since then the distortion and manipulation of religious principles which have been employed in the service of narrow political ideologies will further contribute to cynicism in the British community about our religious beliefs. In any case the R.E. teachers are mostly non-Muslim and therefore present Islam and other faiths and life stances from a biased perspective in their teaching.

There is a tendency to concentrate sometimes exclusively on the outward manifestations of Islam (and other faiths)- places of worship, prayer rituals, pilgrimage, artifacts etc which could deny the deep spiritual values, experiences and meanings underlying these outward and almost superficial aspects of the faith.

This together with the already distorted image of Islam constantly re-enforced through over-simplified books in English written by non-Muslims (and some Muslims), with the best of intentions no doubt; and the effects, intentional or unintentional, of 'Christian' orientated education and or so called neutral secular 'modern' education on the unsuspecting, impressionable young minds is a major cause for concern.

Other efforts under the name of 'Multicultural Education' which have been trying to change the ethnocentric (Eurocentric/Anglo Saxon) curriculum content, and promote better intercultural appreciation and celebrate the rich diversity of cultural differences are similarly rejected as tokenistic either because they create another set of stereotypes to replace old racist or ethnocentric ones, or else because they are seen as peripheral to the central issue of justice and equity. They do not change the structures of oppression which are upheld by the inertia built into any institutionalised form of control and they do not change racist attitudes prevalent in our society.

The nature of discriminatory obstacles placed in the way of establishing voluntary aided Muslim school, which are discussed later on in this paper, is a form of institutional oppression usually defined as "racism". There appear to be such strong 'anti-Muslim' feeling that even the Church of England applications for more voluntary aided school are denied just in case this is used by Muslims as a lever towards asking for their own voluntary-aided schools. This has meant that even the Church which could well be an ally ends up wishing us less than well.

The absence of British Muslims in positions of responsibility within local and central government would either suggest that we are all less able or that there are discriminatory practices inherent in the 'traditional' institutionalised procedures which prevent equal opportunities for members of the second largest faith community in Britain.

If there was enough goodwill, understanding and willingness to support Muslim pupils and students in their efforts to do their best for the greater good of society, on the part of non-Muslim teachers, headteachers, Governors, members of the local SACREs (Standing Advisory Councils on Religious Education), Inspectors/Advisers, Education Officers and locally elected councillors, then both the 1944 Education Act and the 1988 Education Reform Act allow for positive interpretation of the law. For example, schools could take advantage of the GCSE Religious Studies (Islam) syllabus (Mode 2) prepared by the Muslim Educational Trust (MET) and approved by the Schools Examinations and Assessment Council (SEAC). The recent initiatives to establish the studying of Islam as a major option within a B.Ed. degree course at Newman and Westhill Colleges in Birmingham and within PGCE full and part time courses at the Institute of Education in London will begin to provide teachers with these 'shortage' skills and knowledge, but it will need interculturally skilled managers within the education system to deploy these newly qualified teachers in order that all members of the school community benefit from their presence. The need to avoid narrowly defined job descriptions must be obvious. By concentrating their efforts on preparing, developing or producing appropriate teaching and learning materials or translating and interpreting in community languages, without examining the wider framework within which this work is being done, could prove counter productive.

As mentioned earlier, local Muslim communities have for a considerable number of years been providing 'Education' for their children in Supplementary Schools within mostly very inadequate conditions but there have been no formal links between the two providers of 'Education' to our Muslim children.

LEA state schools and the Supplementary 'Schools' have gone their own ways usually. Each of them is generally considering the other in the poorest light possible and giving the children very different value system to sink or swim by. There often isn't any formal contact between the school and the local Mosque or the Muslim organisation.

This non-contact fosters some strange and unhappy situations. For instance in those LEAs where some single sex schools have been retained after comprehensivisation a large proportion of the teaching staff could well be inclined towards creating an anti-sexist or feminist ethos in the girls' schools. The Muslim parents who often go to great lengths to send their daughters to such institutions will have very different reasons for making their choice. This creates a real dilemma in that there are different expectations from the staff and parents. The unintentional consequence of such a situation with real value conflicts put the girls at greatest risk, both socially and emotionally. What may one ask is the purpose of our schools? Is it to serve the needs of parents? teachers? or pupils? The 1980 Education Act may well have much to contribute towards answering these questions. Both central and local government never tire of giving prominance to the role of the parents and the school community. Recent legislation confirms this position. At the moment however, the National Curriculum Council (NCC) or the Local Education Authority (LEA) and ultimately the school teachers decide what is the 'best' curriculum diet for children. Muslim parents and their Islamic perspective on education is either ignored or not taken seriously. It must be said though that in some selective instances the contribution of Muslims have been acknowledged, valued and appreciated. Where such mutual respect exists misinformation which generaly permeates the educational literature has helped to improve things at the margins. On the whole education is unquestionably imposed on children in a most dictatorial manner with a great deal of moral and intellectual arrogance.

V The Response of the Local Education Authorities

As indicated earlier the LEAs and schools are at the moment responding to these 'problem' orientated concerns as 'problems' associated with 'them'; the foreigners, the aliens, the immigrants or the ethnic minorities. Much of this response is of a pragmatic nature and mostly dealt within the context of a very negative atmosphere. None of these policies has really been pro-active in establishing long term objectives in a positive and constructive way in consultation with Muslims.

To begin with the pressure in the sixties was from the indigenous 'white' population who did not wish any school to be 'overpopulated' by 'them'. LEAs took the assimilationist approach within a monocultural system in those early days and got involved in programmes of compensatory provision on the basis of special needs eg English as a Second Language which actively promoted the mono-cultural transmissions in separate language or reception centres. Bussing was preferred by some LEAs to contain white pressure. We then had a period of 'research' and an examination of the multiracial school populations began to 'discover' the socio-economic disadvantages that the 'racial' minority groups suffered. By this time pressure groups had moved the debate on from an assimilationist to an integrationist one. There was also a marked contraction of capital which 'forced' the government towards stronger immigration control. The idea was to control the 'integration' and create harmony between 'races'. Then came the LEA responses on 'multicultural' education. These are still the most commonly favoured policies and strategies which are based on the principle of equality and the celebration of cultural pluralism. This assumes that if you know about 'their' cultures you will be less discriminatory but it does not address the basic problems of religious, linguistic or other forms of racism based on the colour of one's skin.

This historical perspective has moved from LEA responses which were entirely thought out from the perceptions of the immigrant or race problems by white middle class educationists with no real knowledge of Muslims or Islam, to policies created after some research from an ex-colonial perspective into the presence of Muslim immigrants in our cities and finally from the perspective of non-Muslim policy makers in consultation with some Muslim representatives. Some LEAs began to involve ethnic minority communities before responding to their needs. Examples of these LEA responses have been illustrated here from:-

a)   ILEA circular No 81/156 entitled "Guidelines on Muslim Pupils" issued in September 1981.

b) The Bradford Local Administrative Memorandum (LAM 2/82) entitled "Education for a Multi-Cultural Society: Provision for Pupils of Ethnic Minority Communities", issued in November 1982.

These include issues like:-

i) **School Assembly** - Parental right to withdraw children from non secular assemblies on written request and after consultation.

ii) **Islamic Festivals** - Muslim pupils permitted to take days off on the occasion of Eid-al-Fitr and Eid al-Adha and School Governing Bodies to consider taking occasional holidays on these days if possible.

iii) **Friday Payers** - Older Muslim children being allowed to attend Friday congregational prayers (Jum'ah) at the Mosque. Alternatively a room at the school being made available for this purpose and ablution facilities made available where possible. Also in consultation with the Local Muslim Community representative, an Imam being allowed to come and lead the prayers.

iv) **Swimming** - single-sex provision being made with appropriate staffing and the girls being allowed to wear 'costumes' which conform with the Islamic requirements. Shower and changing facilities being made available separately and in single cubicles.

v) **School Uniform** - Muslim girls being permitted to wear trousers (*shalwar kamiz*) and a headscarf provided they are chosen to be in accordance with normal school colours.

vi) **Curriculum** - Muslim parents after consultation with headteachers being allowed to withdraw their children from Music, Dance, Sex Education and any other activity which does not conform with the Islamic requirements.

vii) School and Community - Good co-ordination and effective channels of communication being established between the school and the community with improved translation, interpretation services in appropriate languages. Information to parents about the school being similarly made appropriately available.

viii) **'Halal Meals in School'**
In September 1983 Bradford Council became the first LEA to formally introduce the provision of 'Halal' meat dishes twice weekly in some of its schools. There has been considerable coverage by the media of this issue especially because of the efforts of a persistent minority animal rights group who argue that it is cruel to kill animals without pre-stunning and that the Islamic method of sacrifice (that is what a Muslim does everytime the life of an animal is taken) is more painful than the other method prescribed. This protest goes on and in the local press particularly it has revealed the worst sort of prejudices and racist attitudes.

These bold and innovative responses were applauded by the British Muslims but the feed back so far in terms of implementation of such policies has been far from encouraging. The abolition of ILEA and the changing political control in Bradford have both contributed to the total ineffectiveness of the monitoring envisaged by all those who worked hard to bring about these policies. There remain pockets of good practice wherever committed individuals refuse to be pursuaded that such sensitive and responsive activity is no more than a passing fad.

Headteachers and others who display such positive attitudes continue to gather the fruits of their efforts and make progress towards improving the quality of mutual trust, and gain co-operation from the families of the children for whom they provide an education service.

VI Voluntary-Aided Muslim Schools

During the year 1982/83 Bradford based Muslim Parents Association (MPA) submitted an application to the Bradford LEA to establish five Voluntary-Aided Muslim Schools in two existing First Schools, two Middle Schools, and a single sex girls' Upper School.

The LEA followed the DES Regulations and the procedure laid down in the 1944 Act and the inevitable conclusion was a rejection of that application on the grounds that:-

a)   MPA was unsuccessful in proving that there is a need for such schools in Bradford.

b)   that the entire community, more particularly Muslims of Bradford, were opposed to the scheme.

c)   MPA did not possess the financial resources which may be necessary to run these schools; and

d)   MPA was unable to prove that it should be regarded as the representative voice of Bradford Muslims.

It was also said that if such a scheme were accepted it could affect the future of education and race relations in Bradford adversely. 'White' teachers in these schools had announced that they would leave the service in the event of these schools becoming Muslim Voluntary-Aided Schools. 'White' children and their parents indicated that they would leave these schools.

This process made Bradford LEA more alert to the wider implications in terms of the social fragmentation that

191

might breed further ignorance, fear and violence.

The public debate during the processing of the MPA's application revealed that there are many complex issues closely related to 'Racism' in all its various forms which must be tackled seriously before the issue of Muslim Voluntary-aided schools can really be debated in public.

It was interesting that the then Chairman of the Education Committee Conservative Councillor Peter Gilmour lost his seat in the 1984 local elections seemingly because he took such a bold stand concerning most of these issues. If this was the result of a backlash some of his opponents predicted, it is inevitable that other elected representatives and other LEAs have thought twice before taking such initiatives. The successful blocking of that application together with other factors like the 'Rushdie' affair, the Gulf crisis etc, has strengthened the resolve of the secularist and other lobbyists to such a degree that central and local government refuse to give this issue the importance that some British Muslims feel it deserves.

The right to establish voluntary-aided schools is enshrined in the law of the land. Inspite of seven years of effort by the Islamia Schools Trust, out of nearly 5000 voluntary aided schools costing the Department of Education and Science (DES) a total of £93,339,000 during 1991/2 alone, not a single one is meeting the needs of Muslims. A strong, mostly secular lobby has convinced the Government that they should not allow Islamic voluntary-aided schools, thus denying Muslims the rights that they have in law. The arguments against Islamic voluntary-aided schools have been well rehearsed. Even the Commission for Racial Equality (CRE) considers that they could prove potentially harmful to both the Muslim and the non-Muslim communities. Other arguments can be summarised as follows:

1) 'Voluntary Apartheid' might go against the interest of

the Muslims by 'ghettoising the Muslim Community' (NUT 1989) thus facilitating discrimination against Muslims in the Labour Market.

2) It is a threat to "the stability and cohesion of society as a whole". It might provoke a "racist backlash" (SWANN, "Education for all," 1985 and Asian Youth Movement). It might exacerbate the very feelings of rejection and of not being accepted as full members of society which they seek to overcome. (SWANN)

3) The presence of Muslims in multi-racial schools is needed to help the majority ethnic community to shed their racist tendencies. (SWANN)

4) Stubbornness in conforming to the norms and values of the dream world of a multicultural pluralist Great Britain which may or may not be realised in the next century. (It is claimed that just and rational compromises are shunned by the orthodox/unreasonable/estremist Muslims who have the audacity to demand their legal right in OUR country without wishing to integrate or assimilate.)

5) The best way to meet the needs of the Muslim community is to provide single-sex state comprehensive schools rather than voluntary aided schools.

6) The best way to make progress is to persuade the DES and LEAs to develop policies which take account of the needs of a culturally plural society.

7) The existing denominational voluntary-aided schools must be encouraged to think of closing down in the name of pluralism and unity within a culturally diverse society like ours.

8)   If Muslim and other voluntary-aided schools were established this would deny many of our children the opportunity to share their schooling which is an excellent way to increase mutual respect and understanding.

9)   Voluntary-aided Muslim schools would deny Muslim children the opportunities of a broad and balanced curriculum, diminish their life chances, create ghettos, isolate Muslim girls even more than they are already, drop the 'standards' of education, and could create another Northern Ireland situation here.

What is forgotten is that most of these logical arguments either assume that all Muslims are incapable of running a school which can provide an enlightened form of education with a pluralist perspective or else it is assumed that firstly all LEAs will provide an education which is anti-racist and responsive to the needs of a culturally plural society and secondly that all faith communities at present running their own voluntary aided schools will listen to this splendid point of view and close them down in favour of non-denominational secular state schools. This is the position most of the members of the SWANN Committee took, but 6 members of the committee signed a note of dissent (including myself). It is significantly the only note of dissent in the whole of the 800 pages of the SWANN report[7].

If and when the education system really responds in an enlightened form, as outlined in the SWANN report, to cultural pluralism there will be no need for separate schools of any sort. It seems obvious to the British Muslims today that this emphasis on an ideal future is being used as an excuse for not responding positively to the legitimate legal rights of a minority community.

The result of all this is that the views of the majority (non-Muslims) are forced on a minority. The perceived needs of this minority could well be realised much more constructively if a variety of solutions and practices were allowed to coexist so that individuals and communitites may achieve their different objectives without either infringing upon each other's rights or harming the general interest. The DES and LEAs could use their influence to encourage plurality in a setting which ensures equality of access to public funding and national resources.

The Secretary of State for Education refused an application from Islamia Primary School in 1990 on the grounds that there were already too many places available for these children within the existing schools in the district. When one witnessed the establishment of City Technology Colleges (CTCs) by the Government with no apparent regard to the number of places available in those areas, it is hardly surprising that Muslims consider the refusal to offer positive assistance in establishing voluntary-aided Islamic schools in accordance with the 1944 Education Act or their own community schools with public funding as unjust and racist.

The establishment of Muslim voluntary-aided schools could provide invaluable experience in tackling the real issues and offer the LEAs an opportunity to work closely in partnership with the Muslim community. Such a gesture would be seen as a tangible act of recognition of the rights of Muslims. The overwhelming desire of a minority faith community can and should be respected within our pluralist democracy.

VII Conclusion

It may be useful to reiterate some of the main points which Muslim parents in Britain have voiced over the past three or four decades. It is my feeling that the vast majority of Muslims would agree that this is what they would wish to say to those in charge of providing an educational service to their children:

1)   You must enable our children to become secure in their cultural heritage and faith commitment.

2)   You must offer our children a clearly defined sense of morality and social responsibility.

3)   You must encourage in our children a positive sense of self identity, self confidence, sensitivity, awareness and value orientation which would make them appreciate the need to contribute towards a pluralist democracy like ours.

4)   You must allow our children to explore the cultural diversity (within and beyond the Muslim community) to enrich their own lives and have a balanced view of themselves within a multicultural world.

5)   You must widen their horizons and thereby allow them to experience a sense of liberation, a sense of joy, a sense of awe in appreciating the ultimate and unique gift of life and exercising the full use of the gift of an intellectual capacity without creating a sense of alienation and without feeling a sense of superiority or inferiority in themselves or in others.

6)   You must offer Muslim teachers and educationalists an opportunity to develop a balanced curriculum appropriate for British Muslim children and to share their ideas and experiences with others in the mainstream education system.

7)   You must give the British Muslim community a direct involvement in the future development of the type of

educational provision best suited to the needs of British Muslim children in a non-Muslim pluralist democracy.

8) You must offer the same and equitable right which exists under the 1944 Act to all British faith communities which may help to create and develop trust between the Muslim community and Local and Central Government. This partnership is a vital step which could eliminate many of the blockages restraining change towards mutual understanding.

9) You must empower the British Muslim community in order that they may have reasonable control over their own lives and that of their children whilst at the same time safeguarding children from any misguided zeal of over-anxious extremist parents.

Finally, if schools try to meet the special (but not separate) needs of our Muslim children and involve the Muslim parents more positively in the running of the schools even as they are, much of the frustration would, I feel sure, disappear. Closer links with the supplementary classes (run by Mosques and Madrasahs) are essential if we are to meet our children's needs more realistically. Recruiting, training and retraining Muslim teachers, Muslim cultural liaison officers, Muslim nursery nurses, Muslim (bilingual) classroom assistants and Muslim staff within the educational services to take on pastoral and liaison responsibilities should help enormously. Provided all of us (Muslims and non-Muslims alike) think positively about each other, I feel sure that we can help all our children broaden their horizons and enhance their understanding of a variety of religious beliefs and practices thus offering them an insight into the diversity of values and concerns of different communities which are now part of our society.

197

Notes

1. Ummah: Arabic for the global community of Muslims.
2. Sunnah: A complete record of the Prophet Muhammad's (peace be upon him) sayings and deeds is preserved in the 'Hadīth' and the practice of these 'ways' is Sunnah.
3. Al-Ghazzali, The Book of Knowledge - Kitab al-'Ilm in *Ihyā' 'Ulūm al-Dīn*-translated by Nabi Amin Faris,1962, Sh Muhammad Ashraf Publishers, Lahore, Pakistan.
4. Sharī'ah: The rules and regulations according to which Muslims organise their individual and social behaviour - Sharī'ah is the Law of human conduct.
5. Madrasah: Arabic term for the provision made for groups, usually in the vicinity of the Mosque and usually by scholars of Islam.
6. Black - A global term which is used to politically describe solidarity between minority groups who have a skin colour other than 'white'.
7. *Education for All - The Report of the Committee of Inquiry into the Education of Children from Ethnic Minority Groups.* Chairman: Lord Swann FRSE - Cmnd 9453. HMSO March 1985.

Christian Education and the Maintained School System

Kevin Nichols

I

The Christian Church's relationship with education is foreshadowed and typified by Paul's experience in the Aeropagus. On the one hand he felt called to share his beliefs – his saving and life-giving vision – with all men. So he must accommodate it to the minds of others. He must cast it in concepts and arguments which would be, at least to some degree, familiar. On the other hand, he felt uneasy stepping outside his own categories: the salvation history, the concrete, colourful imagery of Hebraic thought. Having failed once to make a mark among the philosophers, he tried it no more.

Although a few early Christian writers, such as Justin, wrote "apologies" in which they set out their faith in a publicly reasoned form, these were by no means typical of early Christian thought and education. Much more typical was the catechumenate. In this process, applicants, attracted by curiosity or by example, were led through a long process of ritual, instruction, and trial, to an initiation into the mysteries of Christian faith, as these were embodied in the sacraments. The catechumenate was not at all characterised by the light, reason, and dialectic of Greek learning. It set up no stall in the market-place of human argument. Much more it resembled, at least superficially, the

199

pagan mystery religions in which similarly a long and many-sided process of initiation led to a spiritual and personal rebirth.

The events which followed at the heels of Constantine's conversion deeply changed all that. Christianity as the official religion of the social order had to be publicly expressed. It became open to questioning and criticism. It undertook massive conversions and the hasty baptism of innumerable citizens of the empire. It had to come to terms with the public institutions of that empire, among them -- so far as it had been developed -- the institutions of scholarship and education.

Nevertheless, the approach of Christian scholars and catechists to education was a cautious and ambiguous one. Some would have kept converts away from the Greek schools on the grounds that intellectual sophistication could only muddy the clear waters of simple faith. Jerome's *Quid Athenae Hierosolymis* – though coming strangely from so great and versatile a scholar – typifies this view. But others thought differently. Converts of education and ability might be encouraged to go to the Greek schools. If properly prepared they would know how to make the necessary discriminations. They might even "despoil the Egyptians" and bring Greek learning in some way within the Christian fold. The theological justification of this view is expressed in the words of Clement of Alexandria that "there is one river of truth and two streams which flow into it from this side and from that. One is the stream of secular learning, the other, the word of God, the loveliest thing there is." Clement's viewpoint prevailed and brought Christian faith within the commonwealth of learning and within the world of public education.

During the dark ages it was Church which preserved what could be salvaged of the old learning. Consequently it found itself in the powerful position of not only acknowledging the value of education but of effectively controlling it. Nevertheless, the tensions which the Fathers of the Church perceived did not wholly disappear. The massive socio-religious edifice of Christendom contained them but they would emerge again substantially in the same form. Surely, it would be said, education is a risky business for Christians to engage in. For how will simple faith fare if men's mind are possessed by critical reasons? But others would answer: man is a rational animal. Reason is the most distinctive of God's gifts to him. In the open market the truth of Christian faith will prevail. J. H. Newman's *Lectures on University Education* offer an illuminating instance of this tension. The earlier lectures elevate liberal education and its product the "philosophic habit" to great heights. "It is almost prophetic from its knowledge of history; it is almost heart-searching from its knowledge of human nature; it has almost supernatural charity from its freedom from bitterness and prejudice; it has almost the repose of faith because nothing can startle it."[1] Yet in mid-stream he seems to hesitate and change direction. Perhaps the possessors of the philosophic habit will become proudly self-sufficient and thus annihilate their faith. They may become "victims of an intense self-contemplation."[2]

This tension had its counterpart in the world of education itself. Forces there chafed against ecclesiastical control and in due course education freed itself from that. After the French revolution it became plain that a secular idea of education was possible. The establishment of a secular educational system in the United States rested on the support of religious freedom. For within it no set of beliefs could be publicly imposed. Families and congregations would be free to go about the business of religious upbringing in the private sphere where it properly belongs. It marked the beginning of the emancipation of education; the growth of an idea of it which did not require the transmission of a cultural heritage or of traditional beliefs but which established itself on the learning of skills and on initiation into the various ways of knowledge and experience.

The social history of Britain is not characterised by radical fractures. Although in the course of the nineteenth century the need for a national venture in education became obvious, few people advocated that the slate be wiped clean and a fresh secular start be made. In the formative years of the national system, the churches remained dominant. However, the government approached its arrangements tolerantly. Grants should go not only to the established church but to any church which could prove itself able to use them. The Roman Catholic church vigorously set about providing itself with an educational system. So did some of the free churches. Thus from the beginning of the systems education here had to take account of pluralism in belief – even though this appears from our standpoint to have been a pluralism of narrow scope. The government accepted that religion would be part of both educational government and educational content. It accepted that even within the Christian tradition beliefs varied. It adopted two solutions to this problem. There would be a dual system in which the churches would be allowed to maintain their own schools. But in the system there would also be publicly owned schools. In these religion would continue to be taught, but a way must be found for doing this which would be generally acceptable, an agreed syllabus.

The Dual System was a pragmatic concordat, born of historical circumstances rather than political or religious principles. The churches which had the greatest stake in it had also different reasons for defending their position. Anglicans were very conscious of their position as the national church, keeper of the national conscience. Religious teaching "according to the formulations of the Church of England" was, apart from its sensible and moderate orthodoxy, the faith upon which the social and moral stability of the county rested. Roman Catholics, on the other hand, saw themselves as an embattled minority. A system of schools would enable them to survive and thrive. Moreover, the teaching of their church at the time was rigorously orthodox and exclusivist. It was the time of the First Vatican Council and the definition of papal infallibility. The Catholic Church saw itself as a fortress of truth and orthodoxy in a sea of doctrinal error and moral chaos.

Although the original arrangements were pragmatic the concordat had deeper implications which appeared in due course. A school responsible in one direction for secular subjects and in another for religion is possible when its work is envisaged as simple instruction. But when a more sophisticated concept of education is accepted it becomes impossible to prise one subject out of the school's whole task and exempt it from that concept. Moreover, the case for church schools rests partly on the idea that religion as a school subject makes explicit values and beliefs which are implicit in the whole life of the school. If this is so, then the school must be answerable to the church for the whole of its life. Equally, since the concordat requires that a common idea of education be accepted, the church school must in some way be accountable to the responsible authority for its religious lessons. So the church school today rests upon a notion of dual responsibility for the whole of its educational work. In the second section of this chapter I will consider whether such a concept is defensible and feasible. In the third I will offer Christian viewpoint on religion in the curriculum of the maintained school.

II

A thorough assessment of the arguments for and against voluntary aided schools lies beyond the scope of this paper. My concern is with those which affect the character of religious education specifically. So I leave aside the argument that the Dual System is a source of social conflict, which is, in any case, a matter for empirical investigation. Nor, I think, need I discuss the argument that pluralism of beliefs in our society should be mirrored by pluralism within the education system. If this meant that wholly different concepts of education should be allowed to flourish within the same system, that would indeed pose a serious problem. If a group wished to open a voluntary aided school where conditioning or brainwashing was to be practised, that would be completely outside the understandings on which the Dual System is based. But I do not think that is true in the case of any of the Christian churches at present. They, if anything, tend to accept too uncritically the concept of education which is proposed to them. Religious education as a subject is sometimes an outsider to this general acceptance – or appears to be so. However, I shall return later to the argument that a common concept of education will be embodied variously in the different areas of knowledge and experience. There are certainly some complex difficulties involved in the effort to characterise religion as a form of knowledge or a realm of meaning. In spite of these, a case can be made out to justify a different style of education in voluntary aided schools.

In saying this I certainly do not wish to support the view mentioned in the last section; that in a church school, religion as a classroom subject should be excluded from the educational canon on the grounds that it is the church's business, not that of society. This seemed a practical compromise when a simple model prevailed. It is difficult to justify when schools are set public, comprehensive educational goals to which all subjects in the curriculum are expected to contribute. The churches like the rest of society have the right to criticise these goals and endeavour to change them. But this must be done through public concepts and arguments and not by the assertion of private convictions. At this level, the whole system depends upon consensus. It should be added that this requirement applies only to what is done within the official curriculum. What occurs within school but outside the curriculum is another question, though a real one.

I turn now to a second argument frequently used to recommend voluntary church schools. This comes in its most extreme form in the words of Pope Pius XI: "The whole of the training and teaching, the whole organisation of the schools must be so impregnated with the Christian spirit under the guidance and motherly vigilance of the Church that religion comes to provide the foundation and culminating perfection of the whole system."[3] This position is open to the charge of overkill. If explicit religion so saturates the school then what remains of education at the end is no more substantial than the smile on the Cheshire cat. Yet not only is education an autonomous concept and activity, the disciplines and forms of knowledge on which it is based also have their rights. Newman writing of theology and liberal knowledge remarked, "Knowledge is capable of being its own end ... and this is true also of that special philosophy which I have made to consist in a comprehensive view of truth in all its branches, of the relations of science to science of their mutual bearings and their respective values."[4] Forms of knowledge relate to each other, influence each other, even depend on each other. But it is not the business of religion or theology to go trampling over other people's gardens.

However, this argument from "total education" is usually couched in more moderate terms. When supporters speak of the "ethos" or "atmosphere" of a voluntary school, they mean that the belief on which the school is established penetrate actively into many aspects of school life. So it is argued, personal relationship, attitudes to order and discipline, extra-curricular activities, even the curriculum itself, should have a distinctive character on account of the way in which human life is perceived and understood. It would be extremely difficult to test this ethos empirically. Still we ought to look seriously at such an idea of implicit religious education and at its implications for overt religious education too.

We do not here need to consider the school's extra-curricular life extensively. I think most people would agree that a legitimate purpose of church schools is that education should go on there within a community which tries to embody the values and beliefs of its faith. There are problems about getting successfully from beliefs to relationships and arrangements. There are also problems about allowing for freedom and dissent. But these are not in our direct line of argument.

The curriculum, however, is another matter, since it represents the school's formal, public educational commitment. It seems strange to speak of a "Christian curriculum" if that means one constructed of Christian math, Christian history, etc., though attempts to devise one have been made in the past. Moreover, in my view, the autonomy of the forms of knowledge would make such a project dishonest. There is, however, another concept of a Christian curriculum which has more to recommend it. This rests upon the character of the general curricular aims of the school as a whole. These, it is argued, should bring into relationship, without distorting, the specific disciplines. They should rest, as Newman said, upon a "comprehensive view of truth .... the relations of science to science of their mutual bearings and their respective values". Such a comprehensive view in our day appears a chimera. Knowledge on the whole, in education, is viewed rather relatively, rather pragmatically or even as a social construct. However, the theory of knowledge argued by Bernard Lonergan offers some support: arguing not a static unity in the Aristotelian/Thomist manner, but a dynamic unity through the invariant structure of insight:

"The immobility of the Aristotelian ideal conflicts with developing natural science, developing human science, developing dogma and developing theology. In harmony with all development is the human mind itself which effects the developments. In unity with all fields, however disparate, is again the human mind that operates in all fields and in radically the same fashion in each. Through the self-knowledge, the self-appropriation, the self-possession that results from making explicit the basic normative pattern of the recurrent and related operations of human cognitional process, it becomes possible to envisage a future in which all workers in all fields can find in transcendental method common norms, foundations, systematics and common critical, dialectical and heuristic procedures."[5]

No one would expect teachers in church schools to put the matter in quite that way. Still one might expect Christian teachers to have, even in an imperfectly developed, patchy way, some unifying vision of truth. And in the light of this, the division between subject-disciplines would be less marked, their "mutual bearings and respective values" more emphasised. Positive relationships between subject departments, a greater and more imaginative effort for inter-disciplinary work, might characterise a more defensible idea of a Christian curriculum.

Such curricular principles would include in their scope religion as a school subject. Should the inner logic of that subject itself differ from that of other subjects? Certainly it may differ in point of prestige and importance. R. E. teachers in a church school might reasonably expect their subject to be treated as a major one. But it is not obvious that the subject should stand on different foundations. Some argue that it should so stand; they inveigh against treating religion "just like any other subject." What is usually meant by this is that the purpose of a church school is to present the teachings of the church concerned as true, rather than explaining and recommending them. Again when this is probed it usually turns out that the word "true" means factual, like the facts of physics; indeed more true but in the same line of truth, since proceeding from God's revelation not from human investigation. This practice is not defensible against a canon of education conceived in terms of initiation and critical autonomy. The reason is not that propositions may only be taught with a degree of certainty proportioned to the strengths of the evidence that supports them; as though there were some universal evidential calculus. The reason is that the practice rests upon a mistaken view of religious understanding. For understanding varies and evidence varies according to the form of knowledge in which it is embodied.

In practice this mistake is rarely made. The most common practice I believe is to teach the tradition, give reasons for it and promote critical reflection on it with the aim that students may apprehend and accept the tradition personally. This practice might be thought to fail the educative test for two reasons. First because, being narrow, it will fail to develop understanding of the world of religion. I do not think this argument is very strong for this approach may gain in depth what it loses in breadth. The second reason is that in this practice, the tradition is not regarded as reviseable in principle within the intention of the teacher (though he may acknowledge that in *fact* revision may be the result of his method). But education, it is argued, which aims at a critical autonomy would be as open to rejection of the tradition as to the retention. On the other hand, this is an approach which allows for critical thought and which therefore cannot be ruled out of court. Its defensibility I think will depend upon the nature of the critical reflection which it encourages.

This may appear if we compare this approach with education in religion; a style of religious education which aims to promote a thoughtful, empathetic, critical understanding of the world of religion. At first blush it seems that teaching a tradition with reasons and with the promotion of critical reflection differs from this only in scope – education *in* religion draws from several religious traditions. Yet – in the Christian understanding of the matter – the idea of "teaching the tradition" involves two important differences.

The first concerns the connection between religious understanding and its moral requirements. If religion is viewed in the phenomenological way, its moral element appears as a discrete and separate dimension. However, if a whole tradition is to be taught, its several dimensions relate to each other, are connected together in a close and sometimes complex way, are to be understood only in each other's light. An element which appears as one thing when extracted from its context for analysis and comparison – "pinned and wiggling to the wall"– appears as something quite different when seen as part of a living and developing system. In the Christian tradition moral commitment is seen not as a consequence following in the wake of understanding and assent, but as part of the act of religious understanding itself. It is the readiness to follow out the moral imperative in the system which jerks the whole system into a unity; which alters the relations of its elements by making them the interacting parts of a living whole. In the doctrinal area it is not quite clear how a willing suspension of disbelief differs from assent. Equally in ritual, it is hard to discriminate between the experience of going through the motions with sympathy and understanding and worship itself. But the difference between an understanding of moral rules and attitudes and moral action is plain. It is here that the crucial difference between commitment and neutrality lies. It is hard to see how a teacher who does not, in principle, have this moral commitment can be said to hand on the tradition. Of faith in relation to morality, Newman writes: "It is itself an intellectual act, and it takes its character from the moral state of the agent. It is perfected not by intellectual cultivation but by obedience. It does not change its nature or function when thus perfected. It remains what it is in itself, an initial principle of action; but it becomes changed in its quality as being made spiritual." To this word "spiritual" as it is used in education I shall return shortly.

Secondly, this style of religious education as handing on a tradition, however critically, involves itself with conversion. I say "involves itself with" for I do not intend to argue that it should aim at conversion in an evangelistic way. And I understand conversion in Bernard Lonergan's sense as "a change of direction and indeed, a change for the better. One frees oneself from the inauthentic. One grows in authenticity. Harmful, dangerous, misleading satisfactions are dropped. Fears of discomfort, pain, privation have less power to deflect one from one's course. Values are apprehended where before they were overlooked. Scales of preference shift. Errors, rationalisations, ideologies fall and shatter to leave one open to things as they are and man as he should be."[7] In this understanding, conversion is a single mental act, realised at the cognitive, moral and religious levels. It might however be argued that the commitment envisaged here is simply commitment to the truth in religious matters, not to a particular tradition. Indeed conversion does demand that. Hence the requirement that tradition be handed on reflectively and critical autonomy promoted. "Errors, rationalisations, ideologies fall." Still, this should occur in a way appropriate to religious understanding. Hence a tradition is not offered only to be sampled or learned about. It is offered to be participated in a living whole whose component elements interact. This counterpoint of participating acceptance and critical review implies a tradition which grows and develops; and which does so through the process of reflection and enquiry exercised not only on the tradition but also on the whole range of human experience. This is the main function of theology which, rather than philosophy of religion, serves as the foundational discipline of this style of religious education. In this form of knowledge, theology provides the categorial concepts.

In the light of this argument what can be made of the word "spirituality" as in the requirement of the 1944 Act that attention be paid to the spiritual development of the child? So far as it is a legitimate educational word, I believe that it means the activity of critical reflection in the religious field and in a manner appropriate to that field. So its characteristics will include enquiry and the assessment of evidence; though "evidence" here will not be seen as a pale reflection of empirical or mathematical evidence. It will also be characterised by a concern for conversion, in Lonergan's sense. The awakening and promotion of a search for religious truth and authenticity may take place within a religious tradition such as the Christian one. For in this tradition, no religious expression however weighty and authoritative is ever fixed and final. Each one looks to a reality beyond the formulation. Spirituality in this case also includes active participation in the tradition, especially through liturgy and reflection on human experience and its relation to the expressions of the tradition. In theory, the voluntary aided school will be religiously homogeneous. But every religious tradition has its degree of belonging. The construction of a religious curriculum which allows for these degrees of belonging presents a difficult educational task; as the extra-curricular religious life of such a school presents a difficult pastoral one.

III

What kind of religious education do Christians think appropriate for schools which are not aided but fully maintained? Some (not all) of the considerations put forward in the last section have a bearing on this question. Spirituality as I have described it might find a place in this form of religious education; though this is a matter which requires a great deal of further investigation, and from many angles. Equally, Lonergan's account of conversion might play a part. For conversion does not necessarily occur within a particular tradition. Religious authenticity and the search for truth occur and grow in persons who have inherited no religious tradition or who have rejected one. But if they are to count as religious they must follow the defining characteristic of the religious form of knowledge. At least it appears from these considerations that the debate between neutrality and commitment is not so simple as it is sometimes made to appear.

There is one school of Christian thought which maintains that because this is a country of Christian tradition, a fully committed Christian religious instruction should be given. The weakness of this position seems to me to be that it rests upon a cultural even sociological premise. No one would doubt that this is a country of Christian tradition. But all that this would justify is the teaching of the culture. There is no justification for jumping from this to an education resting upon and aimed at personal commitment; unless it can be shown that the two are necessarily connected. But in fact, cultures and traditions continue to exist even though a large proportion of the population does not give personal assent to the beliefs embodied in them.

What do Christians make of the approach usually called "education in religion"? This is the view that what should be promoted is a sympathetic insight into the several dimensions of religion drawing not on one but on a variety of the religious traditions which we find in the world. The usual argument against this position is that religion can be taught only by insiders. Commitment, it is said, is necessarily linked to understanding. The teaching of Islam or of Christianity by non-believers inevitably leads to distortions and mistakes. I have already said that I think there is some substance in this argument though not in the form in which it is usually proposed. Its force lies in two rather different considerations. The first is that the process must be religiously serious; it must be based on the structure of the religious form of knowledge. Hence, as I have suggested, moral commitment seems inescapable. However, it is not necessary that this commitment be to the moral principles of a particular religious tradition. It may be in a less defined way, a moral commitment to the demands of religious truth. So a teacher who works in this style should be a religious person. He should be in Lonergan's sense a converted person: someone who is committed to religious authenticity and the search for religious truth.

Secondly, I cannot see much ground for separating out the dimensions of religion and studying them through instances drawn from the whole spectrum of religious traditions. Indeed it is when this is done that the distortions and errors complained about occur. Elements in a system interact with each other, mesh, support and affect each other. They stand in each other's light. Hence one element which is isolated from a system may appear very differently and may well be wrongly understood. Something which has a function within a system may be unintelligible outside it. Newman put the matter in these words: "I do not forget that the same doctrines as held in different religions may be and often are held very differently, as belonging to distinct wholes or forms . . . and exposed to the influence and bias of the teaching, perhaps false, with which they are associated."[8] So "education in religion" requires sympathetic insight into whole systems, not only into parts of them. I am sure how badly these requirements would undermine the principles and practice of education in religion. Not I think fatally. There are clearly practical difficulties in dealing with systems rather than dimensions. Still the practicability of this approach has always been one of its weaker points. It requires, it has been said, teachers who understand deeply all the religions of the world. It may be enough to say that more than one tradition be studied and that one of these be the Christian, since that is in our national tradition.

Finally, there is a very different Christian view of religious education which is put forward by Edward Hulmes. He takes as his slogan Martin Buber's words: "speech from certainty to certainty, though from one open-hearted person to another." This warns us that the philosophy on which this position rests is not likely to be conceptual analysis. Still it is heartwarming to hear commitments presented in this way. Where neutrality is the watchword, it is argued, where commitment is under the ban, the agnostic is at an advantage. For the presupposition is that religious offerings are highly dubious and start the race with a severe logical handicap. I do not think this is altogether true. I have already argued that a religious teacher should be a religious person though not necessarily in the commonly accepted sense. There are, however, two difficulties about this position. Hulmes argues that in religious education we should put forward our religious convictions boldly and be prepared to put them at risk. But it is difficult to see how, if this is done, the vulnerability of children can be protected. What would be a very bad risk in a Cambridge Combination Room may be a powerful and unquestionable influence in a rural comprehensive school.

The second difficulty is an epistemological one. How can this process be educational in the sense of being grounded in some form of knowledge? It might be argued that it would look sounder against the background of

Philip Phenix' *Realms of Meaning*. It would be synnoetic knowledge, the form which is inherent in personal relationships. Paul Hirst has made criticisms of the realms of meaning as an epistemological basis for education to which I cannot at the moment see an answer.[9] Still arguments could be drawn from Lonergan's view that insight has an invariant structure in all instances, including religious and presumably, personal one. All knowledge is personal, wrote Newman, with the difference between real and notional assents in mind. It was, writes J. M. Cameron[10], in these aspects of his lifelong reflection on the nature of religious understanding that he foreshadows the writings of Kierkegaard.

Notes

1. Newman J. H. *The Idea of a University*. Longmans Green 1947 p 123.
2. Ibid p 171.
3. Pope Pius XI *Divini Illius Magistri*.
4. Newman op. cit. p 91.
5. Lonergan B. J. F. *Method in Theology*, Darton Longman & Todd 1972 p 24.
6. Newman J. H. *University Sermons*, S.P.C.K. 1970 p 249.
7. Lonergan op. cit. p 52.
8. Newman J. H. *Grammar of Assent*, Longmans Green 1889 p 251.
9. Hirst P. H. *Knowledge and the Curriculum*, Routledge & Kegan Paul pp 56 ff.
10. Cameron J. M. *The Night Battle*, Helicon Press Baltimore 1962 p 243.

Conclusion

Syed Ali Ashraf

Christian and Muslim academics have discussed in this book the relationship that they feel cannot but exist between religious beliefs and the content and organisation of education in all branches of knowledge. As education means, as Paul Hirst has stated in the introduction, the imparting of or handing over of knowledge that is considered worthwhile to the next generation, and as knowledge cannot but have an impact on the total personality of those being educated, the authors have tried in this book to explore how far the religious experience of life and the relationship between God and human beings can provide educationalists in two branches of knowledge, Social Science and Natural Science, with principles and a methodology of approach that must not be ignored.

This book has shown that in the religious approach there is a concept of human nature which asserts the presence of something more than ordinary Reason as the main source of cognition, especially in literature and social sciences and the moral dimension of the human personality. Similarly, the scientific world view, based on the work of Reason and sense-data needs to be placed in a deeper and wider perspective that realises the grasping of truth by that aspect of the human self that takes us into a far richer and deeper sphere of the universe in which the spiritual and moral aspect of the human being plays an inevitable role.

We consider this book to be an important step in this field in which Christian and Muslim scholars are working.

Philosophers are also exploring the possibility of stepping outside the current western scientific outlook in order to see it in its spiritual perspective, to see not merely 'further in a horizontal direction' but also in 'the vertical direction' as Huston Smith puts it in his book *Beyond the Post-Modern Mind.*

If this book, *Religion and Education*, rouses in the minds of readers the desire to go beyond the present world views, including the modern scientific world view, to see the world through a mind freed from the narrow concept of logical reasoning, then I think it has fulfilled its primary job.

Appendix

Syed Ali Ashraf

Faith as the basis of Education in a Multi-Faith, Multi-Cultural Country

The papers published in this volume were given as lectures in 1983. Though some of the papers have been updated because of contemporary references, we decided to publish the book because the conceptual discussion remains as it was.

Within these eight years the Islamic education movement has gained new impetus through various research projects. The Islamic Academy has formulated curricula in Social Studies and Natural Sciences.

The work of the Farmington Institute in Oxford, the newly founded Christians in Education, and the new Christian Schools Campaign, indicate that the religious groups have speeded up their activities.

As I realised that the secularist attitudes and views are in all branches of life, and secularists occupy key positions, and as it is not possible even to make the case for religion heard, it is necessary to bring together all the religious groups so that we can stand on a common platform and work positively for the benefit of humanity.

In cooperation with the Department of Education of the University of Cambridge, the Islamic Academy Cambidge organised two seminars - one in 1989 and one in 1990 on *Faith as the Basis of Education in a Multi-Faith, Multi-Cultural Country*. At the former seminar a dialogue took place between Christian and Muslim thinkers, and at the latter there was a detailed discussion among Hindu, Buddhist, Jewish, Muslim, Christian and Sikh educationalists. The document that came out of the second seminar is an important landmark. Hence we are including it in this Appendix.

The purpose is not to form a syncretic religious approach, but to indicate that whatever the doctrinal differences among religions, there are in nearly all religions, common beliefs regarding human nature, God, and a framework of eternal values. Religious groups should stand together so that the complete destruction of these values does not take place in the process of social change.

This document suggests ways and means of not only redesigning the curriculum to include the religious perspective, but also of implementing it. That is why it can be an important step forward from the stage of theoretical discussion, to the practical implementation stage.

FAITH AS THE BASIS OF EDUCATION IN A MULTI-FAITH, MULTI-CULTURAL COUNTRY: DISCUSSION DOCUMENT II

Preface

The importance of education is undeniable. By it our society passes on the intellectual and cultural treasures of the past. Through it our young are prepared for their future. On its success depends to a large extent the moral quality of life open to our citizens and the economic prosperity of our nation. It is not surprising therefore that education's call upon the national and local financial budgets has become enormous and that pupils are being encouraged to spend longer and longer periods at school and college. Similarly, legislative regulations and administrative provisions have become progressively more complex in an attempt to improve quality and raise standards. The subject has moved firmly to the top of the political agenda.

However, education is a value laden activity. Before we can improve its quality we have to be sure that we know what direction it ought to take and what attitudes it should help engender in the young. It therefore becomes a legitimate and important educational question to ask, "What values ought to inform the educational enterprise and help to shape its purposes?"

In previous centuries it was the values of the Christian religion which often infused this country's education. Indeed, up until the beginning of the twentieth century it was the Christian churches who were the main providers of schools in Britain. Even now up to a fifth of the school population spend part and in some cases all of their school careers in educational instituions with some kind of religious connections. Yet nowadays the religious perspective on education often goes by default. There are many reasons for this. Part of the explanation is to be found in the secular attitudes of many of those who fomulate educational policy and practice. Part can be attributed to the spirit of the age with its emphasis on materialistic goals and aspirations and to the consequent decline of institutional Christianity. And part may be due to the past successes of the Christian enterprise which has embedded in our society many of those values which are now taken for granted but whose religious roots have been forgotten.

This country has changed in another important way. We now recognise that we live in a pluralist world in which no one religion or ideology is dominant. Even more significantly, our own residents now include large numbers of adherents of the whole range of world religions. Yet many of these feel alienated by the dominant secularism and legitimately aggrieved that, whilst there are various types of Christian schools, there are no equivalent religious based schools to which they can send their children. It was in the light of this new situation that a group coming from the various major faiths present in this country met to ascertain if there were any values which we all shared, which would more adequately encapsulate afresh in a pluralist society the religious perspective on education and which could help to transform the schooling we provide for our young.

In the discussions which followed it was soon apparent that, in spite of wide differences of religious belief and practice, there were many values which were held in common and which had important implications for the whole educational enterprise. We were especially alive to the subtle ways in which materialistic and selfish attitudes can undermine a more morally sensitive and spiritual appreciation of life, and how the responsibilities and obligations of a common citizenship can be forgotten in the pursuit of personal advancement of private gain. Compassion can too easily be sacrificed on the altar of efficiency.

Obviously we recognised that we share many of our values with other people who do not espouse a specific religious view of life and who are not connected with any institutional religion. We accepted the importance of co-operating with those who thus share our values for the common educational good. Nevertheless we felt it essential to set out the general shape of an approach to education which reflects more fully the religious point of view and to indicate something of its consequences for educational practice.

In doing this we do not wish to advocate a return to the past in which one set of closed presuppositions are replaced by another. We wish to be sensitive to the views of others and to recognise the importance of personal integrity and individual responsibility. Yet at the same time we want to place the discussion of values at the heart of the educational enterprise. Not every participant of our seminar would concur with all that follows, nor would they as individuals always express their own educational convictions in the same terms as those set out below. Nevertheless, it was agreed that the following statement should be offered for

221

further discussion and comment in the hope that this would help forward the important task of framing more satisfactory educational policies for the schools of this country.

A. THE SOCIO-CULTURAL DIMENSIONS OF EDUCATION IN BRITISH SOCIETY TODAY

1. British society today

1.1 Its plural character

British society today consists of diverse groups of people belonging to different religious faiths and none, and a variety of social and cultural traditions and value systems. Even though the influence of the majority group may inevitably be dominant, the plural character of our society is an inescapable fact of life and needs to be acknowledged if a proper analysis of our condition is to be made.

1.2 The role of faith in the major group

Though institutional Christianity has declined, opinion polls report that the majority of the population still call themselves Christians. Too much should not be read into this. But it is evident that religious culture and folk religion are widespread. And even though there is much agnosticism, only a minority explicitly call themselves atheists.

1.3 The role of faith in the minority groups

Muslims, the largest religious minority, Jews, Hindus, Sikhs and Buddhists have come from many different regions of the world. They are all basically faith communities.

2.   Beliefs and Values in British society
In spite of doctrinal differences the various religious groups share some common beliefs and values which could provide these groups and even our society with a means of achieving unity in diversity in areas such as educational policy and practice. These include:

2.1 Belief in a Transcendental Reality, i.e. a Reality that transcends all limitation that particular qualities impose upon an object. With the exception of the Buddhists they believe this Reality to be the Essence of the Being whom they worship and whose name in English is 'God'. Buddhists do not deny the presence of God, yet neither do they affirm Him. But they too believe in the transcendental character of truth.

2.2 Belief in the existence of the spiritual dimension in each human being.

2.3 Belief in eternal and fundamental values, such as Truth, Justice, Righteousness, Mercy, Love, Compassion and care towards all creation. These values are to be found reflected in the human self and need to be encouraged, nurtured, refined and developed so that such seeds may grow, flourish and blossom.

2.4 Belief in the need for Divine (or Transcendental) Guidance. There is a conflict between selfishness and selflessness in each individual, a conflict that is also mirrored in societies, races, states and groups of people. Human beings, therefore, need some norms which transcend race, colour and groups. These norms human beings receive

from the Divine Source and though divinely inspired people.

3. Secularist Vis-A-Vis the Religious Approach to Life

3.1 The basic philosophical difference

The secularist approach to life, on the other
hand, is based on concepts which deny or reject or
ignore the above four religious beliefs either
directly or indirectly. It is an approach which is
instead based on the following ideas:

(a) Human beings are physical creatures that
have come into existence through a physical,
biological evolutionary process from godless,
causeless, completely non-rational, inert
matter. In other words, secularist philosophy
fails to explain how this inert matter acquires
intelligence, feeling and imagination. Religion does not of course deny physical reality,
but believes that the God-gifted spirit of man
is an impingement of the Transcendent Self
on inert matter and that intellect, intelligence,
will and consciousness are the products of
that spirit. Hence when in death the spirit is
separated from matter, these elements are
lost.

(b) Influenced by modern scientific rationalism,
secularists believe in the supremacy of human
reason and treat the human ability to think
logically as the best means of finding the
truth. Human beings are seen, therefore, as
essentially thinking animals. Whilst religion

recognises the importance of reason it rejects an over-emphasis on its powers to solve the deepest questions that confront humankind. Religion also considers that feelings must play a significant role in human life, not only as subjective experiences, but as a means by which through love of Truth, Justice, Mercy and Righteousness, such qualities can be grounded and nourished in both personal and social life.

(c) Secularists often stress material progress and achievements yet find it difficult to believe in the intuitive realisation of truth coming from a transcendent source.

(d) The source of values of secularist philoso-phies is very different from that asserted by the religious approach to life. This affirms that since God or the Transcendent is the Source of values they must be eternal and part of the structure of reality. Indeed they are ingrained in the human spirit and this ex-plains why even small children can possess a sense of justice and an appreciation of truth, love and beauty. It is by cultivating such feelings that human beings can overcome and transcend personal selfish interest. Se-cularist philosophies, however, make social interactions the source of values and so con-sider that all values are relative to historical period and social situations. This inevitably leads to conflicting philosophies of life and cultures and so to a denial of anything called eternal Truth.

3.2 Basic differences in the consequences of religious and secularist approaches

Secularism generates uncertainty in the name of freedom, whilst faith in God can give a new strength to the moral fibre of a person's being and enable him/her to resist those forces which lead human beings to selfishness, cruelty, debauchery, dishonesty and other forms of corruption. This power to resist evil ought to be strengthened, but secularist attitudes can easily weaken it because they underestimate the importance of the interiority of human life and depend too much on externality. But before we can resist evil we must discern what is evil. This is an internal act. Hence the education of the interior is a necessity which the secularist philosophy all too often ignores.

3.3 The importance of the motivation of faith

The objection can be raised that the various faiths have themselves been the cause of violence and cruelty. This has tragically occurred when they have lacked a proper human motivation and stressed differences in formula rather than their internal unity. Once a common motivation is achieved through a common understanding amongst faith-groups that our adversary is this total secularisation leading to the losses mentioned above, we ought surely to be able to construct a common educational philosophy based upon a common starting point - the totality of the human being in whom spirit, heart, intellect, reason and senses work in co-operation and in unison. We ought also to be able to provide pupils with those necessary skills of discernment which will enable them to distinguish what is in tune with the true spirit of religion and what is not.

They would need to realise that:

(a) Commitment to one's own faith ought to make the individual more able to appreciate other faiths and respect them.

(b) The development of religious belief and practice is admirable so long as such a commitment does not adversely affect the freedom and rights of others or limit human dignity.

B. EDUCATIONAL RESPONSES

1. The dominant response today: the secularisation of education

1.1 The secularisation of society and education

Though the churches were at first the main providers of education in this country, the state gradually took over an increasing share of educational provision and in doing so supported a largely neutralist approach to questions of belief and values so far as religion was concerned. Today this approach is dominant. It is argued that religious beliefs are essentially controversial, and since our society consists of diverse groups with varied beliefs and attitudes to life, including those who espouse a secular way of life, education ought to be neutral about such controversial matters. It should be such that it can provide a common basis for all these varied approaches to life and be open to all children irrespective of creed or ideology, facilitating their critical appreciation of and personal decision in relation to these contrasting beliefs and life stances.

1.2 Secularist theories of education

The dominant theories of education that lie behind recent formulations of educational policy are almost entirely rationalistic in tone. Education is seen as initiating pupils into intellectual traditions which are autonomous creations of human beings, each with its own logically distinct modes of thought. They can be carried on without reference to religion, and indeed can provide instruments which can be used to make judgements about ideologies including religions. Similarly values are free standing. They may express the accumulated wisdom of humankind, but they are essentially man made. They do not have, nor do they require, and religious foundation.

2. Rejection of the complete secularisation of education

2.1 The condition of society: its roots

As suggested earlier, British society has its roots in long established religious traditions, and this applies both to the majority and the minority groups. Nor does the existence of religious variety and doctrinal differences exclude the possibility of formulating a common approach to education. As the previous discussion has shown, there is sufficient agreement to allow a common approach to be articulated. The present dominant secular and materialist approach to education in many LEA schools ignores this possibility and implies that we ought to accept a non-religious bias in education which it misleadingly describes as neutrality.

2.2 The secularised system is reductionist

As explained earlier, the concept of human nature which the secularised system embodies tends in practice to be relativistic, individualistic and atomic, and too easily eliminates ideas of religious faith and spirit.

2.3 It promotes 'doubt' rather than 'faith'

It dissociates spiritual cognition from the intellectual realisation of truth and elevates discursive reason above all other forms of understanding, so creating doubt in the minds of pupils about the validity of an affective and religious response to reality.

2.4 The values it espouses lack a sufficient foundation

It cannot and has not provided a secure and coherent basis for a common set of values which any educational system requires.

3. The consequences of a faith-based education

3.1 It prevents religion being marginalized in education.

3.2 It recognises the need in education to grasp the relationship between the material and spiritual worlds.

3.3 It offers a holistic approach to the curriculum.

3.4 It provides a secure basis for a common set of values which could inform the whole curriculum.

3.5 By providing a recognised framework of values or norms whose truthfulness and goodness are affirmed by the faiths because they are bedded in Divine Reality, it would enable pupils to develop in a more coherent way their own individual freedom to think and act as responsible members of their own communities and in society at large.

C. A SUGGESTED COMMON "FAITH" FRAMEWORK FOR THE CURRICULUM

The education here conceived presupposes faith and operates within its sphere, rather than faith being treated as something extraneous to education and external to its major objectives. It therefore sets forward an approach to education which reflects the presuppositions of faith. Nevertheless, it recognises that there will still be those who will prefer a totally secular education. Such should be free to pursue their own goals. For this approach eschews any form of indoctrination or compulsion in religion. A faith which is to be deep and enduring must be chosen and/or held in freedom. As Judaism, Christianity and Islam (and other faiths) believe in one Transcendent Deity, the existence of absolute values derived from God and the reality of the spiritual aspect of human nature, the following curriculum aims are suggested:

1. BELIEFS AND VALUES
(Cognitive & Affective: Knowledge & Attitudes)

1.1 Awareness of God, the Supreme Being (or the Transcendent as Buddhists would affirm).

1.2 Awareness of the Absolute Values in God's Qualities reflected in the Creation, i.e. Humankind and Nature (or awareness of the reflection of transcendent values in creation).

1.3 Awareness that each individual is a unique human being.

1.4 Awareness that we all can manifest within ourselves the values referred to in A2 and that in this lies our humanity.

1.5 Awareness of the faith, history and achievements of one's own community and the importance of being a member of that community, and the development in each individual of the ability to evaluate his/her own culture.

1.6 Awareness that there exists in the world different racial groups within one humankind. We should, therefore, understand each other and live in harmony, respecting the different and differing customs, values, beliefs and languages of the main cultures of the world and of our own country.

1.7 Awareness that the richness of each community depends on how far it can appreciate and value the achievements of other communities and draw upon them for the benefit of its own existence.

1.8 Development not only of tolerance and concern for the rights and beliefs of others, but a commitment to practical engagement on their behalf on the basis of the awareness that in the eyes of God all have equal rights and are entitled to justice and compassion.

1.9 Development of the capability to see all these cultures in a more global context and to shun all stereotypes be they of race, nation, gender or religion. Avoidance of the danger of being caught up by ethnocentric feelings which are in conflict with the essential religious values which are also ethical and the source of all the principles enunciated earlier.

2. INTELLECTUAL, EMOTIONAL AND SOCIAL (Knowledge and skills)

2.1 Nurturing and development of the powers of reasoning, reflective and critical thinking, imagining, feeling and communicating among and between persons.

2.2 Learning how to maintain, develop and renew (and not merely preserve) the social, economic and political order on the basis of values that are fundamentally derived from great religious traditions and human practice.

2.3 Cultivation and development of the physical well being of pupils.

2.4 Cultivation and development of the abilities of communicative competence both in spoken and written form and through a number of modes including verbal, numerical, mathematical and artistic.

2.5 Awareness of the interplay of permanence and change in the social process so that the roots as described in A1 are maintained, but the transient nature of the human condition and interaction are also understood.

2.6 Knowledge of modern science and technology and an awareness and a critical understanding of their relationship to socio-cultural ethics and the fundamental values to which reference has been made in A2.

2.7 Mastery of scientific and other skills necessary for work and living in modern society.

D. SUGGESTED GUIDE-LINES FOR IMPLEMENTING THESE CURRICULUM OBJECTIVES

1. The aim is to equip growing young people with an inner understanding of the basic relation between knowledge and faith, knowledge and virtue, knowledge and action, knowledge and power, knowledge and wealth, knowledge and the socio-political environment and knowledge and national development.

   If this is done properly they will be able to choose to practise religion with an inner understanding of its spiritual, moral and material significance and act according to the religious criterion of conduct in the individual, social, national and international spheres of their existence.

   They will thus be helped to feel a healthy normal satisfaction in being able intellectually to justify their practice in the light of human beings' relationship with God, other human beings and the natural world.

2. Literature courses should be designed and taught in such a manner that the emotive urges of children

233

and young people become refined through imaginative experience and their creative ability is nurtured. They should also learn how to apply religious norms to the products of the imagination and discriminate between correct and false emotive responses.

3. Natural Sciences and Mathematics courses should be designed and taught in such a way that not only will the students learn to be logical, precise and be able to analyse, generalise and conceptualise, but also come to understand the limitations of science and technology and its hypotheses. They should be enabled to grasp the principles of existence that religion has taught and the role of intuition and imagination in scientific research. They need to be able to understand the relationship between the religious concept of Man and Nature as the reflection of God's Qualities and the scientific concepts and to appreciate the necessity of judging the moral relevance of modern scientific work.

4. The study of society and culture should be presented in such a manner that an insight into relational and environmental processes as envisaged in religion is developed in the minds of the students, their sense of selfless service is strengthened, and they acquire the habit and love of living in harmony with external nature. They will need to learn how to resist ruthless selfishness that corrupts social sensibility and know how to direct science and technology for the betterment of human relationships and the maintenance of the world's ecosystem as envisaged in religion.

5. Students should grow up with an ever increasing knowledge of cultures and civilizations and develop an ability to appreciate them and understand the differences and similarities between religious and materialist concepts and approaches and their different consequences, even though unintentional, and the dangers involved in a loss of humanity and an increase in the mechanisation of human personality.

6. Forms of artistic expression should be taught in a way that embodies the spiritual dimension of life, so that through the development of morally aware imaginative reflection, students come to a deeper understanding of the beliefs and values fundamental to religion.

7. Physical education should be taught in such a way that the encouragement of physical well being is not isolated from the development of mental, moral and spiritual awareness. Only then will it provide deeper insights into the true nature of human life, with its limitations, and the relationship which human beings have with God and with the natural world.

E. THE CONTEXT OF A FAITH-BASED CURRICULUM

A faith-based curriculum could be offered in at least the following two institutional contexts:

1. In religious schools (whether voluntary aided or not) which might include schools shared by different religions (e.g. Christian/Muslim joint schools).

2. Ordinary LEA schools, where a faith-based curriculum might be proposed as a more satisfactory basis for education than the present, which is, in practice, unduly secularist.

On the basis of the above principles and guide-lines a common core curriculum should be framed, present syllabuses should be revised and, what is most important, teachers who are in sympathy with the views expressed in this document should be trained to teach all subjects as having religious presuppositions without at the same time destroying the appropriate autonomy of each subject. If the teachers are not trained, such a syllabus cannot be effectively implemented.

Contributors

Professor Syed Ali Ashraf, Director General, The Islamic Academy, Cambridge; Member of the Faculty of Education, University of Cambridge, U.K. and Rector, Darul Ihsan University, Dhaka, Bangladesh.

Dr. Hasan Askari, Ex-Lecturer, the Centre for the Study of Islam and Christian-Muslim Relations, Selly Oak Colleges, Birmingham, U.K.

Professor Ilyas Ba-Yunus, Department of Sociology-Anthropology, State University of New York, College at Cortland, Cortland, New York, U.S.A.

Professor Paul J. Black, Professor of Science Education, Centre for Educational Studies, King's College, London.

Dr. John Greer, Reader in Education, University of Ulster at Colerain, Northern Ireland.

Professor Paul H. Hirst, Emeritus Professor of Education, University of Cambridge, U.K.

Mr. Graham Howes, Fellow of Trinity Hall, University of Cambridge, and Staff Tutor in Social and Political Sciences at the Cambridge University Board of Continuing Education.

Mr. Akram Khan-Cheema, Senior Education Inspector for Staff Development, Bradford Local Education Authority, Yorkshire, U.K. A consultant for Islamic Education Board, U.K. and U.K. Muslim Education Waqf.

Mr. Stephen Medcalf, Reader in English, School of European Studies, University of Sussex, U.K.

Mr. Peter J. Mitchell, Lecturer in Education, Department of Education, University of Cambridge, U.K.

Dr. Abdullah Omar Nasseef, Professor of Earth Sciences, King Abdul Aziz University, Saudi Arabia; Secretary General, Muslim World League, Makkah, Saudi Arabia; Ex-President, King Abdul Aziz University.

Rt. Rev. Kevin Nichols, Holy Family Presbytery, Co. Durham, U.K.